INDIAN
Christmas

• Essays • Memories • Hymns •

Edited and with Introductions by
Jerry Pinto and Madhulika Liddle

SPEAKING TIGER BOOKS LLP
125A, Ground Floor, Shahpur Jat, near Asiad Village,
New Delhi 110049

First published by Speaking Tiger Books 2022

Anthology copyright © Speaking Tiger Books 2022

The copyright for individual essays, excerpts, hymns and images vests in the respective authors, translators, artists, photographers or their heirs/estates.

Pg. 243 is an extension of the copyright page.

ISBN: 978-93-5447-354-8
eISBN: 978-93-5447-352-4

10 9 8 7 6 5 4 3 2 1

All rights reserved.
No part of this publication may be reproduced, transmitted, or stored in a retrieval system, in any form or by any means, electronic, mechanical, photocopying, recording or otherwise, without the prior permission of the publisher.

This book is sold subject to the condition that it shall not, by way of trade or otherwise, be lent, resold, hired out, or otherwise circulated, without the publisher's prior consent, in any form of binding or cover other than that in which it is published.

Jerry Pinto is a writer and poet based in Mumbai. His books include *The Education of Yuri, Em and the Big Hoom* (winner of the Hindu Prize and the Crossword Book Award), *Murder in Mahim* (winner of the Valley of Words Award and shortlisted for the Crossword Award), and *Helen: The Life and Times of an H-Bomb* (winner of the National Award for the Best Book on Cinema). Jerry's landmark translations from Marathi and Hindi include Baburao Bagul's *Jevha Mi Jaat Chorli Hoti* (*When I Hid My Caste*); Sachin Kundalkar's *Cobalt Blue* and the memoirs of Daya Pawar (*Baluta*) and Swadesh Deepak (*I Have Not Seen Mandu*). In 2016, Jerry received the Windham-Campbell Prize and the Sahitya Akademi Award.

Madhulika Liddle is a novelist and award-winning short story writer. She is best known as the author of the Muzaffar Jang series, about a 17th-century Mughal detective. She was the first Indian to win the Commonwealth Broadcasting Association's Short Story Competition (2003). Her novel, *Garden of Heaven* (2021), is the first of four novels that will span 800 years of Delhi's history.

Jag mein pyaar ki khushboo lekar
aaye Jesus
happy Christmas

(Jesus has come to earth
And made it fragrant with Love.
Happy Christmas.)

—Ataur Rahman Tariq

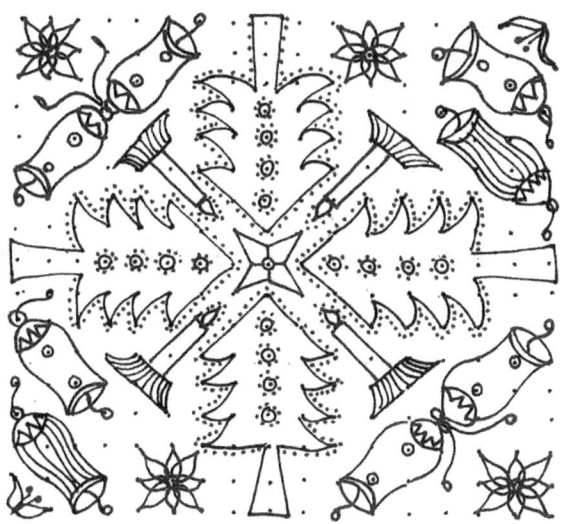

A Christmas kolam design.

Contents

*

Introductions	13
Unto All of Us a Child Is Born	13
Jerry Pinto	
Christmas in Many Flavours	20
Madhulika Liddle	
1. The Child: A Poem	27
Rabindranath Tagore	
2. Gadariyon Ne Dekha Ujaala Aadhi Raat (At Midnight the Shepherds Saw the Light)	31
3. Cake Ki Roti at Dua Ka Ghar	33
Madhulika Liddle	
4. Calcutta, Teri Christmas Pe Qurbaan	48
Mudar Patherya	

5. Poems for Baby Jesus 52
   Arul Cellatturai

6. A Merry Vindalee to You! 56
   Anupama Raju

7. A Christmas Wedding in Kottayam 63
   Elizabeth Kuruvilla

8. I'm Dreaming of a Goan Christmas 73
   Vivek Menezes

9. Gaon Ki Khushi Alag Hai 85
   Mary Sushma Kindo

10. My Memories of Christmas 92
    Hansda Sowvendra Shekhar

11. In Search of an East Indian Christmas in Mumbai 101
    Deborah Rosario

12. Bombay Blues and Ghosts 115
    Jane Borges

13. Did Your First Christmas Cake Come Out of an Ammunition Box Too? 125
    Easterine Kire

14. Santa Comes in a Rickshaw: Christmas in Bow Bazar 129
    Nazes Afroz

15. Christmas in the Moon Place 141
    Veio Pou

16. Yuletides of Yore: Memories of High-altitude Christmases in Kodai, Valparai and Darjeeling   153
  Minoo Avari

17. A Village Christmas   163
  Damodar Mauzo

18. How India's Pluralistic Past Shows the Way Forward   170
  Manimugdha S. Sharma

19. Christmas Pakwan   176
  Jaya Bhattacharji Rose

20. The Spirit of Christmas Cake   185
  Priti David

21. Armenian Christmas Food in Calcutta   192
  Mohona Kanjilal

22. Christmas Memories of a Family   196
  - A (Sort of) Christmas Miracle   196
    Nivedita Mishra
  - Letting Go of Santa   202
    Rushil Mishra
  - On Growing Up Through Christmas   204
    Fiza Mishra

23. Christmas Boots and Carols in Shillong   208
  Patricia Mukhim

24. The Season of Hope in Chandigarh   217
  Nirupama Dutt

25. Christmas Carols Punjabi Style	221
26. Made in India and All of That *Nilima Das*	224
27. A Christmas Prayer *Words and Music by Alfred J D'Souza* *Arranged for Choir by Leon de Souza*	232
About the Contributors	236
Copyright Acknowledgements	243

Introductions

Unto All of Us a Child Is Born

~ *Jerry Pinto* ~

I remember my surprise when I saw my first live Santa Claus. He was a figure in red that Akbarally's, Bombay's first department store, wheeled out around Christmas week. He was a thin man, not very convincingly padded, and he was in some kind of toy car which he pedalled frantically around the store, waving at bemused children and adults. He was nothing at all like the rotund Santa of glossy greeting cards and storybooks. But within a few minutes I had warmed to him, laughing at his cheerful 'Ho-Ho-Hos', and then laughing with him. He seemed to be from my part of the world, someone who would climb up our narrow Mahim stairs and leave something at the door for us at three or four a.m., then take the local back to his regular job as a postman or seller of second-hand comics. The man in the cards and storybooks preferred London and New York. And a lot of snow.

There wasn't much snow in Bombay, except when someone from the family pulled out an old record of Jim Reeves singing 'White Christmas' and we all listened respectfully because 'those old singers were the best, what voices—you can understand what they're saying, not like this modern noise'. (Where do old songs from the US go to die? They go to Goan Roman Catholic homes and parties.) But since we had seen snow on the Christmas cards that came from cousins abroad, we dutifully unrolled balls of cotton wool and decorated inoffensive young casuarinas, dressing them up as pine trees.

Christmas was about Jesus, yes, and about the Nativity, yes, but it was also about food. Everyone had a family member who had soaked the raisins in the rum when October came around and sent it all to be baked at the Irani down the road which did the honours lovingly. Everyone had a friend who made marzipan with peeled almonds, or who made marzipan with the skins and this was debated every year. Everyone also knew that when the sweets came out, you had to pounce on the good stuff—the milk creams and the slices of that cake with the luscious raisins—or you'd be stuck with the rose cookies and the neoris, which were just plate-fillers.

Quite contrary to public imagination, we did not eat

large quantities of meat. In Bombay, protein was fish for most of the week and on Sundays, we might have chicken. Pork was meant for special occasions, vindaloo and sorpotel being favourites because everything could be tossed into the curry. Only the upper classes had things like pork roast and the pigling with the apple in its mouth.

We also knew that we would go to church on Christmas Day and that the new polycot trousers would scratch behind the knee and the entire building would smell of Old Spice, An Evening in Paris and 4711, the eau de cologne from Maurer & Witz marketed for older women. Those were the days when we used perfume on special occasions, like Christmas. The rest of the time we made do with Cuticura or Ponds Dreamflower Talc. And so, naturally, the parish priest would upbraid us for allowing Christmas to be overwritten by capitalism.

We dreamed through those sermons but often the priest was right. Today, it is almost a cliché to say that Christmas, like every other festival, is hostage to the market.

But just stop for a moment, ignore the demands on your wallet, the shrill cries of the merchant who wants you to spend. Ignore the accretions that occur even in a country where less than three per cent of the population is Christian of any form or persuasion, and come back to the basics.

The central celebration is the birth of a child. There is no culture that does not celebrate this event, because all of us who belong to the human race can see our collective future in the pudgy little face. We marvel at this conjuring act, the miniature miracle, at its tiny fingernails and budlike nose. That life should bring forth life is such an ordinary thing that in general, we do not celebrate it. If we did, we should stop and marvel at the mould that grows on an orange that is past its prime (for us, not for the mycelia which think it delightfully ready), and we should gasp in delight at the sight of moss growing on a wall in the monsoon. All this is life making a bid for the future, thrusting itself forward with no assurance that it will be allowed to continue. But let us forgive our species its parochialism, and let us agree that a human birth is indeed special. The world seems a generous, beautiful place in that moment, full of promise and hope.

But stop a moment—there is a different reason why that birth in Bethlehem moves us so much, year after year. Here is a child in perilous circumstances. His parents are exiles. They are homeless. They are refugees: The Virgin Mary, carrying the child in her womb, bumping about on a donkey, and Joseph—a good man, we are told; when he found his fiancée pregnant, he did not want her stoned to death; he wanted to keep her safe, even before an angel told him the truth of the matter, that she was carrying God.

They knock on door after door and they are turned away. Later, the boy grown to wisdom will say: 'Whatsoever you do to the least of my brethren that you do unto me.' (Beware, you nations that turn the refugee away and build walls to protect the wealth that has been built on expropriation. If you trumpet your Christian beliefs and thump your Bible as you do so often when elections come around, turning the refugee from your door is tantamount to turning away the Holy Family in its hour of need.)

The family reaches Bethlehem, where, by the way, it does not snow and there are no pine trees. As I said, focus on the basics. The family finds that there is no room at the inn but is allowed the use of the stable and there the child is born. The infant is laid to rest in a manger, warmed by the breath of animals.

Word goes out in the form of a new star blazing in the sky. This leads the Magi, the three 'Kings of the Orient' as they are known, to the stable. They bring gold, frankincense and myrrh, thus establishing the gifting tradition of Christmas. They come, they worship, they see that this is something special but they go home to their faith.

And who is the birth announced to next? Shepherds watching a flock by night.

As a boy, I asked my father: 'Wouldn't the sheep have been in the fold at home? And the shepherds asleep?'

My father said, 'They must have been nomadic shepherds.'

I knew of nomads in our own parts, homeless tribes living on the streets, and I understood: the Good News, the Godspell, was first announced to the poor. The savants saw it in the sky as a star. The angels themselves came down to announce the news to the shepherds.

But the rulers of the time were terrified. The star foretold a grim destiny for them and so we have the story of the slaughter of the innocents, all children under two to be done to death to make sure that one threat will be neutralized. I recognized the horror again when I heard the story of Krishna's birth—his mother imprisoned and every baby she birthed snatched from her and dashed to the ground.

Little Jesus survived. Warned by an angel, Joseph took the family to safety in Egypt.

That was the beginning.

When I read the Bible as a boy, the four stories of Jesus broke my heart. They raced so precipitately to his death—even one of the gifts, the myrrh, was an augury of the time when he would be laid in the stone cave during the time between the crucifixion and the resurrection.

Standing at the foot of the cross, witness to the death of her son, his painful crucifixion, was the mother. Her pain greater than his, than ours.

Every birth is special, yes, but I think the birth of Mary's child moves the world to joy and generosity because we all—even those not of the faith—carry the image of the apostle of peace nailed to the cross. His suffering was great; the price he chose to pay so that we would learn to love. He would raise no armies, wield no weapons, fight no wars, but he would turn no one away. It is this knowledge—that love and peace will not be extinguished by rejection, betrayal and cruelty; that the child will become a man who will teach us this lesson for eternity—which makes us celebrate the miracle of his birth as our own private miracle, renewing our faith in life. In humanity. In ourselves.

Every Christmas in Santiniketan, Rabindranath Tagore would give a talk about Christ's life and message. Speaking on 25th December 1910, Tagore said:

> The Christians call Jesus Man of Sorrow, for he has taken great suffering on himself. And by this he has made human beings great, has shown that the human beings stand above suffering.

And exactly twenty-six years later:

> As Buddha offered people his incomparable friendship, he [Jesus] announced not only a scripture, he awakened love in the hearts of many. And in the love is really the salvation.

The miracle child, the Man of Sorrow belongs equally to us all. Unto all of us is Jesus born. Into every heart, in Bethlehem or Banaras.

Bombay/Mumbai
October 2022

~

Christmas in Many Flavours

~ *Madhulika Liddle* ~

According to the annals of the Mambally Royal Biscuit Factory bakery in Thalassery, Kerala, its founder Mambally Bapu baked the first Christmas cake in India. It's said that Bapu, who trained as a baker in Burma, set up the bakery in 1880. In 1883, at the instance of an East India Company spice planter (who supplied Bapu with a sample of an imported Christmas cake, along with some ingredients), he set about trying to create a Christmas cake.

Mambally Bapu's cake is supposed to have contained (among other ingredients) cocoa and dried fruit. Given that baking powder hadn't been invented yet, Bapu used a local brew, fermented from cashew apples and banana, to help the cake rise.

I wonder what that first Christmas cake tasted like; how close to the many thousands of cakes still baked and consumed at Christmas in Kerala? Or for that matter, the many more made across India? Similar to these, I suppose, but possibly with its own distinctive flavour—which, happily enough, might be said for just about any Christmas cake in India. The general impression of a cake, rich in raisins and gaudy tutti-frutti, dark with caramel, and with a distinct booziness to it is all very well, but there are more variations across India than one can count. The Allahabadi version, for instance, uses petha (candied ash gourd) as a part of the fruit component, ghee instead of butter, and adds a generous dollop of orange marmalade to the mix. Maharashtrians add chironji (Cuddapah almond) to their cake; most recipes from Kerala and Tamil Nadu include cashewnuts. The Goan 'black cake' derives its colour from a caramel taken really far.

Our Christmas cakes are a reflection of how India celebrates Christmas: with its own regional flair, its own flavour. Some elements are the same almost everywhere; others differ widely. What binds them together is that they are all, in their way, a celebration of the most exuberant festival in the Christian calendar.

Christmas celebrations, of course, run the gamut from the deeply religious to the relatively secular. On the one hand, there is all that marks the solemnity of the occasion: the birth of Christ. Church services, choral music, and some amount of fasting (the latter only in some communities) fall into this bracket. On the other hand, there's all the merrymaking, the food and drink, the song and dance, even though the song often spans everything from the stirring 'Hallelujah Chorus' to vibrant songs of praise sung in every language from Punjabi to Tamil, Hindi to Munda, Khariya, and Mizo tawng.

Given the many denominations Indian Christians fall into, it's hardly a surprise that Catholics, Syrian Christians, Baptists, Anglicans, Methodists, Lutherans and others all have their own slightly differing ceremonies. Midnight masses and Christmas morning services are common pretty much everywhere, though, and groups of carol singers touring the parish, singing carols at the homes of parishioners, for several days or even weeks before

Christmas, is an integral part of festivities. The singers may carry guitars or dholaks, they may sing a cappella; but all of them can be assured that they will be welcomed into homes, heard, applauded, and fed.

Among the more secular aspects of the Christmas celebrations are the decorations, and this is where things get even more eclectic. While malls, hotels and shops in metros and other large cities go all out with fancy artificial trees, miles of fairy lights and expensive tree ornaments, churches tend to be (appropriately) more sedate: banks of massed poinsettias, potted chrysanthemums, a quietly decorated tree, and a crib—depicting Christ in the manger, with Joseph, Mary, the Three Wise Men, shepherds and sundry cattle—are the usual accoutrements.

It's somewhere in between these two ends of exuberance and expense that other decorated spaces, such as homes and neighbourhoods, come in. Some may be all fancy, with LED lights and imported ornaments; but many more will use paper streamers, a small thuja or araucaria tree, and cotton wool for snow: it all depends. Paper stars, or the lanterns known in Maharashtra as akashkandil, are hung by many outside front doors or on balconies; and, in a lovely indigenous touch, there are families that also add a rangoli, crafted from rice flour or flower petals, on floors. In many homes, a small crib is also included in the decorations.

Cities and towns with substantial Christian populations often make sure there's a good deal of mass decorating, with streets and public spaces being prettied up weeks in advance. States like Goa or Kerala, for instance, decorate and illuminate entire localities. Aizawl, in Mizoram, is hard to beat in this regard: the authorities here have an annual competition for best-decorated neighbourhood at Christmas, with a hefty prize of Rs 500,000 awarded to the winning neighbourhood.

These, it must be noted, are the more urban forms of decoration: rural India has its own norms, its own traditions. Wreaths and decorated conifers are unknown, for instance, in the villages of the Chhota Nagpur region; instead, mango leaves, marigolds, and paper streamers may be used, and the tree to be decorated may well be a sal or a mango tree.

This indigenization of Christmas is something that's most vividly seen in the feasting that accompanies Christmas celebrations all across the country. While hotels and restaurants in big cities lay out spreads of roast turkey (or chicken, more often), roast potatoes and Christmas puddings, the average Indian Christian household may have a Christmas feast that comprises largely of markedly regional dishes. In Kerala, for instance, duck curry with appams is likely to be the pièce de resistance. In Nagaland, pork curries rich in chillies and bamboo shoots are popular, and a whole roast suckling pig (with spicy chutneys to accompany it) may hold centre stage. A sausage pulao, sorpotel and xacuti would be part of the spread in Goa, and all across a wide swathe of north India, biryanis, curries, and shami kababs are de rigueur at Christmas.

Of course, as any self-respecting connoisseur of Christmas feasting knows, it's not just the meals, it's also the snacks. In the West, these may include Christmas cake, mince pies, and the like; in India, barring the Christmas cake (in its varying forms), the range of snacks can be mind-bogglingly vast and calorific. Among the East Indians of Mumbai, for instance, milk creams, mawa-filled karanjis (puffs), walnut fudge, guava cheese and kulkuls are a must. Kulkuls, squiggly sweet fried dough curls, are also popular in Goa (where there are plenty of other snacks as well, mostly served as what is known as a kuswar: a platter of goodies that can include kormolas, gons, doce, and bolinhas—an array of confections, their main ingredients ranging from coconut to chana dal). In Kerala, lacy, crisp rose cookies are popular, as are 'diamond cuts', sweet fried dough, covered in syrup. Diamond cuts, known in Hindi as shakkarpara, are common across north India as well as in Maharashtra; in Maharashtra, they form an integral part of faral, the spread of sweet and savoury snacks, that's so much a part of Christmas feasting. In places like rural Jharkhand, the Christmas cake itself may be replaced by a deep-fried rice flour sweet known as airsa.

There are other aspects of Christmas celebrations. The Christmas bazaars, now increasingly fashionable in bigger cities. The choral Christmas concerts and Christmas parties, the latter often not merely the smaller dos confined to a household and its friends, but big community affairs, with dancing, community feasts, Christmas songs, and general bonhomie. Across the Chhota Nagpur area, tribal

Christians celebrate with a community picnic lunch, while many coastal villages in Kerala have a tradition of partying on beaches, with the partying spilling over into catamarans going out into the surf. In Kolkata's predominantly Anglo-Indian enclave of Bow Bazaar, Santa Claus traditionally comes to the party in a rickshaw, and in much of northeast India, the entire community may indulge in a pot-luck community feast at Christmas time.

This is India. An India where rangolis and kolams, gujiyas and faral, mango leaves and dholaks have all traditionally been part of indigenous celebrations; a land where, instead of wholesale and mindless importing of Christmas ideas, we've been discerning. Where we bring in all our favourite (and familiar) ideas of what a celebration should be, and fit them together into a fiesta all our own. Missionaries to Indian shores, whether St Thomas or later evangelists from Portugal, France, Britain, or wherever brought us the religion; we adopted the faith, but reserved for ourselves the right to decide how we'd celebrate its festivals.

Noida/NCR
October 2022

The Child

A Poem

~ Rabindranath Tagore ~

The final two sections of one of Tagore's finest long poems, inspired by the life of Jesus Christ. Tagore wrote the poem first in English, in 1930, and translated it himself into Bengali the following year, titling it 'Sishutirtha'.

IX

The first flush of dawn glistens on the dew-dripping
    leaves of the forest.
The man who reads the sky cries:
'Friends, we have come!'
They stop and look around.

On both sides of the road the corn is ripe to the horizon—
the glad golden answer of the earth to the morning light.
The current of daily life moves slowly
between the village near the hill and the one by the
river bank.
The potter's wheel goes round, the woodcutter brings
fuel to the market,
the cow-herd takes his cattle to the pasture,
and the woman with the pitcher on her head walks to
the well.
But where is the King's castle, the mine of gold, the
secret book of magic,
the sage who knows love's utter wisdom?
'The stars cannot be wrong,' assures the reader of the sky.
'Their signal points to that spot.'
And reverently he walks to a wayside spring
from which wells up a stream of water, a liquid light,
like the morning melting into a chorus of tears and
laughter.
Near it in a palm grove surrounded by a strange hush
stands a leaf-thatched hut,
at whose portal sits the poet of the unknown shore, and
sings:
'Mother, open the gate!'

'Mother and Child', painting by Rabindranath Tagore.

X

A ray of morning sun strikes aslant at the door.
The assembled crowd feel in their blood the primaeval chant of creation:
'Mother, open the gate!'
The gate opens.
The mother is seated on a straw bed with the babe on her lap,
like the dawn with the morning star.
The sun's ray that was waiting at the door outside falls on the head of the child.
The poet strikes his lute and sings out:
'Victory to Man, the newborn, the ever-living.'
They kneel down, the king and the beggar, the saint and the sinner,
the wise and the fool, and cry:
'Victory to Man, the newborn, the ever-living.'
The old man from the East murmurs to himself:
'I have seen!'

Gadariyon Ne Dekha Ujaala Aadhi Raat

(At Midnight the Shepherds Saw the Light)

Gadariyon ne dekha ujaala aadhi raat
Veh baari-baari galle ki
Karte rakhwaali
Ghabraaye jab ki
Bola farishta aadhi raat

Farmaaya usne:
'Bethlehem tum jaao,
Ki paida hua Yeshu Masih aadhi raat

'Kapde mein lipta tumko
Milega ek bachcha
Ki charni ka bhi
Chamka sitaara aadhi raat.'

At midnight the shepherds saw the light
By turn, they kept watch
On their flocks
And were startled when
At midnight, the angel spoke.

He said: 'Go to Bethlehem,
For there is born, at midnight, Jesus the Messiah.

'There you will find,
Wrapped in swaddling clothes, a child:
For at midnight,
The manger's star too has shone.'

Cake Ki Roti at Dua Ka Ghar
~ Madhulika Liddle ~

In Alwar province of Rajputana, sometime in the 1870s, a couple of teenaged boys were left orphaned and homeless after their family was killed in an eruption of violence. Hasham Singh and Chet Singh, with no relatives to turn to and nowhere to go, found refuge with two Christian missionaries who lived and worked in the area. Robert Liddell and Captain Mathew McCune sheltered and supported the two brothers for the next several years; eventually, Hasham Singh and Chet Singh decided to convert to the religion of their benefactors—and when they did so, they also changed their names, taking on their surnames as well in the process. Chet Singh became Clement McCune and Hasham Singh became

John Alexander Liddle, the 'Liddell' changing to 'Liddle' somewhere down the line.

Robert Liddell, incidentally, came from a family of missionaries, but the most famous of the Liddells was known not for his evangelism (though he did that too) but for his athleticism. Robert Liddell's grandson Eric Henry Liddell, known as the 'Flying Scotsman', was a runner of repute who won the gold in the 400 metres at the 1924 Paris Olympics—his story immortalised in the 1981 movie *Chariots of Fire*.

All of this, I hasten to add, is not too much of a digression.

Hasham Singh/John Alexander Liddle was my paternal great-grandfather. My grandfather, who was his eldest offspring, built the house I always associate with Christmas. In the heart of Mission Compound in Saharanpur, Uttar Pradesh, this house was named Dua ka Ghar: 'House of Prayer', and still stands, a long old house, added to and renovated over the decades, with a wide brick path running between the row of rooms and the high boundary wall.

This path is where the sunlight falls, long and strong, in the winter months. This was where, when we went visiting Dada and Dadi, along with hordes of other aunts, uncles and cousins, we would congregate in the late morning for a cup of tea and some Christmas goodies. I was perhaps six years old, at the most seven; like the other children, I would get milk, not tea. Like the other children, too, I would get the run of the many goodies that had been cooked over the weeks leading up to Christmas.

There would be cake, of course, and baking powder doughnuts. Namakpara, strips of fried savoury dough studded with cumin seeds; and shakkarpara, a sweet version dipped in a light syrup that was then allowed to crystallise. Gujiyas, the crisp pastry enclosing a lightly sweetened mix of semolina, raisins and nuts: no khoya here, no heavy syrup on the outside. My parents tell me that baajre ki tikiyas, thin patties made out of pearl millet flour sweetened with jaggery, used to be a staple at Christmas teatime at Dua ka Ghar; but I have no recollection of those.

What I do recall vividly is the cake ki roti.

Cake, at Dua ka Ghar, used to be baked—at least to a child's bedazzled gaze—by the quintal, or more. When it is made in those quantities, it is well-nigh impossible to make at home, so the family, like most Christian families in north India, would go to a baker. Not for the baker to do everything; no. Whichever family members were designated for the job would visit the bakery, carrying all the ingredients: flour, butter, sugar, fruit, nuts, spices, whatever. Even the lined cake tins. The baker would do the mixing under the eagle eye of the customer, who would wait to see their cakes put into the oven before—if other business called—leaving. By the time you came back, after perhaps three hours, your cakes would be out, cooling, so that you could take them home, to be wrapped in butter-paper and somehow kept safe from greedy children till Christmas.

The cake ki roti was a by-product of that large-scale baking. When you are mixing such huge batches of cake batter, there is usually some left over: not enough for an entire tin, not so little that it can be thrown away with no compunction. The baker would therefore extend this a little: flour would be added into it, and the whole thing worked into a dough. It would be shaped into a large, flat disc and baked till it was golden and biscuity.

The cake ki roti, like the cake, would be wrapped and stored for later. It would not be served to guests; it was too pedestrian. Even for the family's teatime treats, it would not be taken out until pretty much everything else was finished. Steadily through Advent and Christmas, past New Year, we would feast on the cake, gujiyas, doughnuts, namakpara and more. When all of those had been eaten, the cake ki roti would finally be unwrapped and served with the tea (or the milk). It might have a few stray bits of orange peel or candied fruit, perhaps a tiny piece of nut here or there, and it had a faint whiff of the spices that had gone into the cake, but it was not even the ghost of the cake. A mere memory, a hint of Christmas cake.

There was more to Christmas at Dua ka Ghar. My Dada used to supplement his pension from the Railways with income he would get by making Christmas cards and other such crafts—and that money he would use to buy gifts for the children of the neighbourhood, who would come to Dua ka Ghar to celebrate, to see the tree Dada would decorate, to feast and to receive gifts from Dada.

Every evening, too, there would be carols. Not the staid 'O Come All Ye Faithful' or 'Silent Night', but the sort of hearty, exuberant ones that were closer to our collective hearts: *Sun aasmaani fauj shareef* (which is the Hindustani equivalent of 'Hark the Herald Angels Sing'), *Oho Maseeh aaya zameen pe/khushi hoti hai* (The Messiah is here, joy to the world) and *Aaya hai Yesu aaya hai/mukat le saath aaya hai* (Jesus has come, He has come, bringing with Him freedom).

Though we are not Punjabi, perhaps my grandfather's association with the Punjabi missionary Sadhu Sundar Singh had rubbed off on the family, and one of our favourite carols was a Punjabi one, which we always sang with great gusto: *Ajj apna roop vataake/Aaya Eesa yaar saa-de paas* (Today, having changed His form/Jesus comes to us, friend) went the chorus, and even those who could not quite remember all the verses joined in at that with much more fervour than any of those carols composed in distant, unfamiliar lands could command.

This, by the way, has been one of my pet peeves for a long time: why on earth do people think that a religion *must* be associated with a particular space? Christianity may have come to much of India by way of missionaries from Europe or America (not all of India; St Thomas, who brought the gospel to Kerala, was perhaps more Asian than Caucasian), but that does not mean the religion remained a Western construct. By no means; Indians adopted Christianity, but made it their own.

We translated the Bible into our languages. We

translated their hymns, and composed many of our own. We built churches which we at times decorated in our own much-loved ways (I have seen mango leaves decorating St Martin's in Delhi Cantonment; I have seen Mary clad in a blue saree in a Pondicherry church). Our ways of celebrating religious festivals carried, still, a hint of what we knew from our own cultures. I am sure the gujiyas and namakparas, the shakkarparas and bajre ki tikiyas of our Christmas feasts had been what our families feasted on back in the days when we celebrated Holi and Diwali rather than Christmas and Easter.

But thanks to Hindi cinema, popular fiction and a confusion between Indian Christian/Anglo-Indian/European, most non-Christian Indians seem to have got the impression that Indian Christians are somehow just brown-skinned sahibs. That we speak only English and some broken Hindi (or whatever other vernacular). That the women wear dresses and the men, suits. That we eat and drink (and drink, how!) Western stuff. That our dining tables are loaded with pies and pastries, with casseroles and roasts.

When I got married, in 2000, I had not even realised how many of these misconceptions prevail around us. My husband is Hindu and when our first Christmas came around, we drove down to Meerut, to spend it with my parents. My husband, ever the gourmet, chatted with me on the two-hour drive: what delicacies were we likely to get? Christmas pudding with brandy sauce? Roast turkey? Stuffing, roast potatoes, gravy?

No, no and no. I told him—we are not Angrez, you know. Why would we eat any of those things? (Not to mention that you could not get hold of turkey or goose in Meerut, even if you wanted to.) I explained, long and vociferously, our family traditions of food, especially of Christmas food. How even our Christmas cake had a touch of India: one of its ingredients was petha, that super-sweet candied ash gourd so popular in much of north India.

I do not think my husband really believed me; when we arrived at my parents', to be served cake and coffee and ham-and-cheese sandwiches, he looked askance at me, as if calling my bluff. That lasted till dinner: Christmas Eve, with masoor ki dal, rotis, salad, and shami kababs.

Lunch, perhaps, my husband thought: Christmas lunch, with all the trimmings.

And Christmas lunch was mattar pulao, with chicken curry, salad, and a tamatar ka bharta—chopped tomatoes cooked till they are falling apart, then cooled and mixed with chopped onions, green chillies, green coriander and salt. For dessert, there was gajar ka halwa, made of red winter carrots, cooked long and slow in milk and sugar until they were utterly sublime.

It was a standard Christmas lunch for us, and a revelation for my husband.

We have been married twenty-two years now, and my husband knows exactly what is coming up at Christmas. My mother is too frail to do much cooking for large numbers any more, but come Christmas, I carry the family tradition forward. I make shami kababs, lightly spiced with peppercorns and cloves, with green chillies, onions and mint to add some pizzazz. The chicken curry is there. The tamatar ka bharta. The cake (I am the only one in my immediate family who still continues to bake the cake using the recipe passed down by my grandmother, and I bake enough to distribute). Add the baking powder doughnuts.

It is, in a way, a chance to relive my own childhood, somewhat. When my family did not travel to Dua ka Ghar for Christmas, we would celebrate at home, wherever we were, and I always looked forward to helping my mother prepare for Christmas. The heavy-duty work of cutting the peel, the candied fruit, the petha and the walnuts would be left to my father, who also got the job of painstakingly measuring the cake tins and cutting out butter-paper to line them with. My mother would do the (equally heavy-duty) work of mixing the batter for the cakes, kneading the dough for the doughnuts, and making the gujiyas. I would do the fun stuff: standing at the counter beside Mama, I would use a little serrated cutter (rather like a pizza cutter) to press together the edges of each gujiya. Or I would be deputed to cut doughnuts: a small steel glass for the larger circle, an old and well-washed lipstick tube for the doughnut hole.

My father used to be in the Indian Police Service (IPS), and that meant a lot of moving around the country, from Assam (where I was born) to Himachal, to Madhya Pradesh, to Srinagar and more. In a lot of the places we lived, there may have been a small Christian community and a church, but all the elements of Christmas that my parents would have taken for granted in a larger town—Saharanpur in my father's case, Calcutta in my mother's—were not necessarily around. Christmas decorations, for instance, had to be bought on the rare occasion when one paid a visit to a state capital. Candied peel was unavailable, and my mother ended up resorting to DIY, cooking orange peel in syrup and drying it over several days. She got local metalworkers to craft cake tins for her out of old Dalda tins, and, armed with a correspondence course in dressmaking, she made new dresses for us, embellished with lace and buttons brought from Calcutta.

My maternal grandfather had worked many years with the music major HMV, and given that my father was from a fairly musical family as well, Christmas music was an important part of our lives. My parents had acquired a collection of LPs featuring carols by greats like Jim Reeves and Pat Boone, and we would begin playing these on our turntable from a couple of weeks before Christmas. 'White Christmas', 'Silver Bells', 'O Little Town of Bethlehem'—these were the carols I could recognise long before I could read the words to them. My mother, incorrigibly irreverent, would invariably twist a word here or there to turn a carol on its head. Mama it was who also taught us the time-honoured parody of 'While shepherds watched their flocks by night':

While shepherds washed their socks by night
All seated around the tub;
A bar of Sunlight soap came down
And they began to scrub.

When I was about twelve years old, Papa was transferred to Delhi, and suddenly, Christmas too underwent a change for us. Delhi, glittery and more stylish, with far more to offer than the small towns we had been in so far, allowed much more to be done. Our Christmas tree got bigger (my father, always a keen garden, had access to bigger and better nurseries from where to procure araucarias). The ornaments got prettier; an uncle and aunt who had recently migrated to the Gulf added to them. Condensed milk became widely available, and my mother discovered a recipe for chocolate fudge which she added to her repertoire of Christmas goodies. Our LPs gave way to cassettes, and eventually to CDs.

In Delhi, my parents became members of the Cathedral Church of the Redemption, an imposing building of sandstone constructed around the same time as the Rashtrapati Bhawan and the rest of Lutyens' Delhi, to be the church for the British who then lived in this area. Back then, in the 1980s and 90s, we lived less than a ten-minute drive from the Cathedral, and there was time to have a quick breakfast (topped off with a slice of Christmas cake, of course) before going to church for the Christmas English-language service, at 8.30 in the morning. The Cathedral, with its organ, choir, soaring vaulted roof and general air of grandeur, was nothing like any of the churches I had been in so far, but there is—even to this day, when I am no longer a child and no longer intimidated by it—a certain majesty to it, a feeling that carries through even into the fact that the English service is a sung Eucharist: most of the prayers and rituals are set to music, not merely spoken.

After the service, we would flood out of the church, into the lawns and gardens of the Cathedral, to meet family and friends. Amidst much greeting and chatting, there would also be cups of coffee and slices of Christmas cake. The cakes, enough to feed several hundred people, would be provided by the members of the Women's Fellowship, and for me, those cakes were an interesting part of going to church: I got to taste, and to compare, cakes. Some came oozing booze; some had lots of spice, as ours did; some were chockful of fruit and nuts; others were heavy on the caramel, light on the raisins.

We could not, however, stop too long at church, because visitors would start arriving at our home to greet us (and, as many of them frankly admitted, to savour Mama's Christmas cake). More often than not we would get back home from church to find at least a few people—most of them colleagues of my father's, along with their families—waiting. More of them would come through the rest of the day, with my mother, my sister, me and our servant setting up a sort of tea-and-goodies assembly line, to make sure there was always enough to be served to everyone. Lunch was usually ham or egg sandwiches, cobbled quickly together in the rare few minutes when we did not have guests in the house. Our relatives and close friends always came to visit well before Christmas. Or we would go, carrying a cake, neatly wrapped in silver foil and then wrapping paper.

One year, hoping (perhaps) to free up more time at home during the day, we decided to go for the midnight mass at the Cathedral. Mama, who had grown up in Calcutta, remembered wonderfully moving midnight mass services at the Joda Girja (St James' Church, the 'joda' part of its local name referring to the twin towers of the church). She hoped, possibly, that the midnight mass at the Cathedral would be somewhat similar, a solemn and quietly joyful celebration of the birth of Christ.

But we were in for a bad shock: it was, as we later admitted to a relative who asked, 'a mela'. Midnight mass, we realised, had become the wannabe space to be in. If you did not usually attend church; if you weren't Christian but wanted to see what all the fuss was about; if (I suppose) you wanted to boast about the beauty of midnight mass (this was in the days before social media; now, I fear it would be worse)...you went, not for the morning service, but for the one on Christmas Eve. There were hordes of people, the church packed to the rafters, toddlers racing about everywhere, no room to breathe.

That was the first and the last time we went for midnight mass. Perhaps things have changed now; but I am happy going for the morning service. I do not even live in Delhi anymore, but in neighbouring Noida; even then, it is the Cathedral Church of the Redemption we go to on Christmas. Tradition, I suppose, has a lot to do with it.

Tradition, too, which makes me still use my family's old recipes for Christmas cake, gujiyas and doughnuts. Tradition, which means that our Christmas lunch is still mattar pulao, tamatar bharta, and chicken curry, with gajar ka halwa for dessert. It is tradition, too, that we still play (though now on a YouTube playlist) the carols I loved as a child. Tradition that we still get together with my parents, my sister and her family for Christmas.

Things have changed, of course. Our social circle is not a fraction of what my parents' used to be, and given that most people's social lives are now online rather than off, Christmas greetings are exchanged on the phone or on social media. Christmas is now, for us, a much more sedate and quiet festival. That hectic socialising is gone, those hurried lunches of sandwiches are a thing of the past. Instead, after the morning service, we get together at either my sister's or my parents', to exchange gifts, and to have a long and leisurely lunch.

My daughter, now nearly nine years old, was asked the other day in school to write a short essay on 'Your Favourite Festival'. She chose to write about Christmas. The Christmas tree we decorate has also changed. For many years, I used an artificial tree; some years back I switched to creating a book tree: sometime in Advent, my daughter and I get down stacks of books from our shelves—especially the ones with red or green covers—

and erect a roughly conical tree on a table that I drape with a red tablecloth. The gifts we begin to choose and buy several months in advance, and my daughter helps me to wrap and label them. The cakes I bake, with her somewhat inept help, given that all she really wants to do is make a mess. The doughnuts she cuts for me, using the same steel glass I used for this task forty years ago (that glass has acquired the status of an heirloom).

Every year, too, my daughter ends up learning Christmas carols at school. When she was tiny, it was the predictable 'Jingle Bells' and 'Rudolph the Red-nosed Reindeer'; over the past couple of years, though, her repertoire has become more varied, more interesting. Last year, for instance, she was taught 'Joy to the World'. And, in what was a pleasant surprise for me, a couple of carols in Hindi. For the twelve days of Christmas, we were treated to repeated renditions of *Door ek taara jaa raha hai/Pahunchega ek din Bethlehem ko* (A star travels in the distance/It will reach Bethlehem one day) and *Mera prabhu janma/pyaara prabhu janma* (My beloved Lord has been born).

It took me back to my childhood, to a simpler, sweeter time. When Christmas was not quite so commercial a festival as it has now become even in India. When it did not matter if the tinsel on our tree was a little tacky, and the tree itself was either a somewhat droopy real one, or a blatantly bright and artificial one. When dholaks and harmoniums were what we heard in church, rather than organs (or infinitely worse, electronic keyboards).

When Christmas had not been so appropriated by the hep and happening that it had lost much of its religious significance.

A child's voice lustily singing *Aage-aage taara/peechhe-peechhe pandit log* (The star leads the way, the wise men follow): such a heartwarming and wonderful reminder of all that Christmas was, and still can be.

Calcutta, Teri Christmas Pe Qurbaan

~ Mudar Patherya ~

My happiest time of the year is usually when it is 359 days old. I could cut happiness out of the Calcutta air with a spoon on 25th December. The winter chill is just right enough for you to wear your winter coat without sweating; whereas if it were Delhi, we might have been numbed into staying indoors and if it were Chennai, it would have been just another T-shirt morning.

The light is magical—diffused, yellow and benign. When I see it slant into my drawing room at 7 a.m., I begin to hear Vivaldi in my head. Calcutta could well be on a ramp walk at Christmas time; even people who live on the streets will find something new to wear—a pointy Santa cap with a cotton ball on top—and shout out 'Merry Christmas' to total strangers.

Interestingly, one of the first impulses in the city of my origin is not about aggregating as much as it is about giving away. On 'burra din', a number of Calcuttans will step out and reach out to the less-privileged—visiting Mother Teresa's Nirmal Hriday with gifts, toys or even a magic show. The kids watch the show wide-eyed or are content to wordlessly hold the visitors' hands.

Decades ago, we would engage one prominent Calcuttan (Russi Mody, Harshavardhan Neotia, Iftekhar Ahsan, or Suvransu Mitra), dress him like Santa Claus, prop him on a buggy and cart it through the by-lanes, scattering sweets from a red bag as the cavalcade gathered a following of dozens of street children yelling, 'Santa! Santa!'

~

There is always the magic of going to the midnight mass at St Paul's Cathedral and returning, stirred by the power the orchestra wields in a resonating cathedral. Or the nostalgic will drive to Bow Barracks to be at the music party where the standard Anglo-Indian line is, 'Come bro, dance, men!'

The hoity-toity will brave the thirty-minute car queue to get into Tolly Club's 24th December night party where every Pretty Young Thing wears black, every second dress ends above the knee and every third is spaghetti-strapped. Every Calcuttan will seek to do a 400 m tawwaaf (parikrama) of Park Street, soak in the lights, buy a Flury's pastry, take a selfie with the giant Christmas tree alongside Park Hotel, hang out at Allen Park's live music event and go home saying, 'What fun we had!'

The slightly older gentry will go to Tolly Club's Christmas Lunch on the lawn where CEO Anil Mukherjee stands at the entrance in his Stetson and tie (!) like Branson welcoming guests at his mansion gate, Michelle belts out 'It's nowwww or nevveh' at 2.43 p.m., some woman with purple hair walks in and well-intentioned folks stretch their necks to stare until their wives nudge them in the ribs, and the buffet comprises orange ginger roast chicken with fennel and radicchio salad, grilled mutton in mint sauce and blanched fish in leek sauce and broccoli mornay for the thirty-third consecutive year.

Everyone in Calcutta—and this includes even conservative Muslims—will call for some rum or rum-less raisin cake and say, 'Bhai, aapko Merry Christmas' (Brother, wish you a Merry Christmas) to each other at this festive time. A number of families in the city also become one again around this time as children return home from universities for their annual vacation.

~

In the past, the Calcutta Test would inevitably be played during New Year's week because no city quite hosted Christmas or New Year as Calcutta did; no city could boast of its unique fusion of the colonial and the Indian so that when the batsman took guard on 1st January there were still snatches of the Christmas lilt floating in one's head; there was dew on the ground and half the stadium was shouting 'Happy Noooyaaar'. There were sandwiches packed into cane baskets; there was a pair of binoculars that would pass through eighteen hands before it reverted to its owner; there was an official leave requested for weeks in advance so that one could watch the match with one's son to educate him on the required 'etiquette'—a sacred rite in the process of cultured evolution where it was necessary to have a perspective on the Vietnam war, communism, the great Bengal famine, Ravi Shankar and, of course, the great post-Christmas Calcutta test match... If Holly Golightly were to have substituted Tiffany's for Calcutta, it would not change her story one bit: 'I am in Calcutta for Christmas. Nothing bad can happen to me here.'

Christmas is also the day I thank Calcutta for a well-rounded secular existence. More than what can be said of other cities in India today. Go anywhere in the country. They may be adding more to the GDP than us guys. But if the good old Mughal can be paraphrased in reference to Calcutta, let me say it loud and clear, '*Gar Firdaus bar rooey zameenasto, hameenasto. Hameenasto. Hameenasto.*' (If there is a heaven on earth, it is here. It is here. It is here.)

Poems for Baby Jesus
~ Arul Cellatturai ~
Translated from the Tamil by Paula Richman

(The Pillaitamil poems form a significant genre of Tamil literature. In these, the poet takes on the voice of a mother and lovingly praises kings, gods and goddesses, and saints as if they are children. Atul Cellatturai addresses the moon in these two Pillaitamil poems, which offer praises to Baby Jesus.)

I. Moon 1

Since you receive light from another source
since you rise high in the sky
while many people watch,

since you receive life again
even though your body dies,

since you remove the darkness of the world
with your light,

since you conceal your vast form
in a round white shape,

since you bear a blemish,

since those who read stars seek you,
since you are appropriate for supplicants/night blossoms,

and since the hero of my poem,
the Lord born of a virgin
who is conceived through the Holy Spirit,
is like you,

Moon in the beautiful sky
you should quickly agree
to play joyously and happily
with the one who is entwined with Tamil poetry,
flowing like a waterfall.

Moon, come to play.

~

Vailankanni Matha—Our Lady of Good Health, Vailankanni.

Moon 3: Difference

You look like a pearl,
but a single smile from my Master surpasses that.

You rise high in the sky,
but have you ever crossed the sky
And seen lofty heavens like my Lord?

You get smaller when your form shrinks,
but my Master has never decreased in size like you

You appear in one direction and disappear in the opposite one,
but he defeats you by going in all eight directions.**

Only half of the time you wander
and then you remove the darkness outside
but all the time, he remains inside us
Don't you know his nature is superior to yours?
Why do you still hesitate?

With this young offshoot of God,**
joined with this budding and flowering Tamil,
Moon, come to play.

With the Son of God,
seated on the right side of Gracious God,
Moon, come to play.

**Eight directions—the eight compass points
**Young off-shoot of God—literally, a leaf bud of God. The little child is compared to the tender, soft, beautiful bud of a leaf. The child is also linked with the tenderness and richness of the Tamil language, which has grown and flourished.

A Merry Vindalee to You!

~ Anupama Raju ~

*B*aby Jesus must have been born in the kitchen. Well, at least as far as my family is concerned. Because for us, Christmas always signified food. Lots of it. The Christmas menu at home usually consisted of the time-honoured fruitcake, chicken fry, beef cutlets, vegetable fried rice and the *piece de resistance*, pork vindaloo.

The excitement of this hearty meal usually started several weeks ahead of 25th December, when my mother bought all the ingredients of the fruit cake from Nilgiris, the large department store on Cathedral Road in Madras (when I reminisce, it is very difficult for me to say Chennai). I knew Christmas was around when the house smelled of the little tutti-fruti, the glazed cherries, orange peel and so on. And then, about two weeks before baking day, she would soak them all in brandy. I hated the cake, much to her irritation, but loved devouring the cherries. Of course, today, I would simply drink the brandy. My brother, on the other hand, not only loved her cake, but also licked up the batter left in the mixing bowl. He still does.

For my father, a Roman Catholic, Christmas meant a trip to Kochi, his hometown. He always said the Kochi markets offered a sweeping range of stars and other Christmas ornaments to choose from, while Madras had limited options. So, after every pre-Christmas trip, he would come back with at least three stars for our home. Since these were from Kerala, they always had a distinct appearance in the neighbourhood. My favourite was the white star with a single long tail.

Other than the star, we had the tree and whenever possible, a crib. I was always the most exuberant one in the family when it came to decorating the tree or making a crib. I envied the churches that created elaborate cribs with real grass, life-size statues of the three kings, sheep, donkeys and of course, the holy family, with a rather unhealthy-looking angel hanging from a tree, blessing the scene. Inspired by all this, I would try to sprout wheatgrass on a small bed of sand, paint scrunched up brown paper to make it look like rocks, and then recreate the nativity scene.

The entire razzmatazz of ornaments, crib and all

came alive on Christmas Eve. As the sun came down, the festive mood would set in, with the Christmas stars lit up, making it all very misty and emotional, adding sparkle to the evening. My father's friends and some of mom's colleagues would drop in for dinner and drinks. But we rarely saw my dad and his cronies. They were all in his office on the top floor and the terrace, drunk as fish, enjoying the food that was sent up for them. The rest of us would be downstairs, having the splendid meal, listening to carols, tired from all the festivities. Since most of Christmas Eve was spent entertaining guests, there was no time for church.

Christmas Day is when we went to church. Lunch was usually just us, enjoying the elaborate affair. And of course, the vindaloo was always the star.

Vindaloo is a popular Goan dish the Portuguese brought to India somewhere around the fifteenth century. Known as *carne de vinha d'alhos*, meat marinated in wine-vinegar and garlic, the dish was adopted to suit local ingredients available along India's west coast. The Konkan coast is well-known for this delicious villain, but on my father's side of the family in Kochi, Mattupurath, vindaloo became something else entirely—something irresistible. In fact, for us, it was reborn as 'vindalee'—as if it were a more feminine version of the 'vindaloo'.

Our vindalee does not use red chillies or potatoes like the traditional dish, but only pepper. And so, the dish is more brown than red. There's also that dash of coconut oil and the flavour of curry leaves, which add a very Malayalee touch to the masala.

Betty aunty, my father's eldest sister; Jessy aunty, who was married to my father's younger brother; and Beebi (Beena, my father's younger sister who I named Beebi for some weird reason): They all made a mean vindalee. However, it was my mother's that almost always won most hearts, if I say so myself. I find it fascinating how she learnt to make the dish though she herself was born a Hindu. She learnt the recipe from Ammachi, my grandmother, her mother-in-law. Apparently, Ammachi sent the recipe on an inland letter, that old, ubiquitous, blue, ancestor of WhatsApp. My mother perfected it over the years. So much so that my father thought she made the dish better than Ammachi.

Pork belly is best suited for this dish, because it gives you the perfect mix of meat, skin and fat. I like the taste of garlic and shallots bathed in vinegar and pork fat the best. The soft flesh of the garlic bulbs, the tanginess of the gravy, the occasional bite of the gingery mustard, are all enough to lift my spirits any day. And if the portion did not include meat, I would still be content with the appealing and aromatic masala.

The most important ingredients for my mother's vindalee are the extra doses of garlic and shallots. While both add a glorious taste to any dish, the most annoying bit about garlic or shallots is that they need to be peeled. I remember my father doing his part by peeling tonnes of them for my mother, a day ahead of Christmas. The translucent skin of the shallots and garlic would fly around like little fairies in our dining room as my father laboured away.

My mother would then slice up the ginger and make a generous paste of peppercorns, cinnamon sticks, cloves, mustard seeds and vinegar. This would be then mixed in with the meat, along with the peeled whole shallots, whole garlic pods, juliennes of ginger, chilli powder, turmeric powder, salt, curry leaves and coconut oil. The magic of the mix lay in hands. Yes, we use our bare hands to rub this paste onto the meat. My mother also recently told me that the bark of a drumstick tree is usually added to the vindalee to tenderise the pork. This could be possibly giving it its silky texture.

A dash of vinegar is added, along with water and the wicked masterpiece is ready to be cooked for about forty-five minutes on a slow fire. And you have your pork vindalee. Like most meat dishes, this one too tastes best the next day.

The vindalee made most frequently at home was the one with beef, but special occasions demanded a pig's life. The beef version is just as appetising, but not as special as its pork counterpart. For one, there is no fat and so, it goes down a notch on the flavour front. Second, the meat is not as tender either.

The dish goes best with hot rice and Jim Reeves. Maybe because ours is a family of musicians and singers, music played a huge role in the season. Jim Reeves was always around at the time, to set the tone. There were no mistletoes or sleigh bells, but there was his rich baritone, warm and comforting like potato soup.

Back in Madras, vindalee still remains a dish heavily

in demand. And nobody waits for Christmas anymore to cook it. It makes an appearance regularly on our dining tables, to warm and tempt us. But I make this tantalising dish only once a year, on Christmas Day, in our home. When that rich, brown, symphony with the pieces of soft meat, garlic mellow like sunlight, shallots soaked in mustard and vinegar, pungent like rain, beckons with its promise of heaven, I know Christmas is here.

Pork Vindalee, Mattupurath-style

INGREDIENTS

- Boneless pork with moderate amounts of fat—1 kilo, cut in cubes
- Peeled garlic pods—1 big cup
- Peeled shallots—1 big cup
- Ginger juliennes—2 tablespoons
- Four green chillies—diced
- Vindalee paste made with vinegar
- Mustard seeds—1 tablespoon
- Pepper corns—1 tablespoon
- Cinnamon—2-3 sticks
- Cloves—4-5
- Vinegar—quarter cup
- Red chilli powder—1 tablespoon
- Turmeric powder—1 teaspoon
- Salt to taste
- Coconut oil—1 tablespoon
- Curry leaves—a bunch

- Drumstick bark—a small piece
- A pair of hands that does not mind the sting of spice—to mix all ingredients thoroughly!

METHOD

Wash the pork well in cold water a few times and set aside in a cooking vessel. Take the ingredients for the paste and grind them smoothly with the vinegar. Avoid using water. Add the chillies, ginger, garlic, shallots, chilli and turmeric powder, coconut oil, curry leaves and salt to the meat. Now mix it all nicely in using your hands for a few minutes till the paste is coated evenly on the pork cubes. Add a bit of water to cook and place it on low flame, on the stove. Close the vessel with a lid and leave it to cook for about forty-five minutes. Every now and then, give it a gentle stir. Once the meat is cooked, let it simmer without a lid for a few minutes, till the gravy thickens. Shut off the stove and let the vindalee settle for some time. Serve with rice. And, oh, don't forget Jim Reeves!

A Christmas Wedding in Kottayam
~ Elizabeth Kuruvilla ~

It is Christmas Eve, 2003. K and I rolled out of Calicut on his Enfield that morning, deliciously late for a change. The kitchen at the Heritage Seaside Hotel where we had stayed the night—the erstwhile Malabar English Club built in 1890—had lived up to its colonial antecedents by serving up perfectly poached eggs for breakfast. The wood-panelled dining room with uniformed serving staff was an appropriately formal space, making me glance nervously down at my forks and knives to check if there were any untamed implements that would betray my nativeness.

K stomped off to tie our bags to the bike's pannier,

a ritual that always attracted a few admiring bystanders, their curiosity heightened by the sight of two dusty people and a Delhi number plate so far down south. Perhaps, they were really trying to figure out the level of barminess needed to undertake such a journey. All packed, K finally flung aside his Gold Flake and kicked till the bike roared in enthusiasm. The heavy jerk with which this machine pulls off never fails to make one feel part of a great adventure.

This was the last day of our ride through the length of the country. We had crossed Rajasthan, stopped to meet friends in Baroda and then Bombay, decided against a full day of riding soon after we left Bombay and entered the Western Ghats to stay at Mahabaleswar, then onto Goa, Karnataka and now Kerala. All that was left was to head naire, naire (straight, straight) to the homestead in Kottayam. That is all the direction we ever got as we went along the narrow, winding state highways, along the edges of which were packed all the buildings and people and trees it could possibly ever hold.

I was the pillion rider, and after fourteen days on the road from Delhi, the trick was to find a comfortable sitting position. I already felt posteriorly challenged, and alternated between lifting myself off the seat altogether to keeping my weight on the right. Having started late, and with no desire to prolong the agony, we focussed on the road ahead. There were Christmas stars hanging from trees in the courtyards of the houses and shopfronts we passed, even more so as we hit the road from Kochi towards Kottayam after a late lunch of parotta and beef curry at a roadside shack. There were more stars on shopfronts, and the windows of one-storey houses. These would all be lit up when darkness fell in a few hours.

I had grown up in Calcutta and then in Delhi, with infrequent trips to Kerala in my childhood. So, this was the second time since we had entered the state from the Karnataka border into Kasargod, which has a sizeable Muslim population, that I would be taken by surprise by the confident presence of communities which, in the north, were largely unseen minorities. There was no ghetto mentality in the women walking down the streets in their burqas in Kasargod. None in the paper lantern stars announcing the arrival of the biggest festival of the Christians in central Kerala. I bet nobody in this state would ever stumble while trying to pronounce what I had, within the first decade of my life, begun to consider my very foreign name.

The hanging of these star-shaped paper lanterns was, I learnt later, not a particularly new cultural import from the West. I had heard from my mother that at Edathua, the village in the riverine Kuttanad area in Alappuzha district which was her maternal home, stars would be fashioned from bamboo at home every year.

We were joining my extended family at Kottayam for Christmas, but that was not the reason we were there. It is our wedding party that is gathering at my paternal grandmother's house. Built over a hundred years ago, this is a house with nooks and crannies waiting to be discovered, and several school summer holidays were well spent, oil lamp in hand for effect, doing just that. It is only when you walk around the outside of the house, peering up at the maroon-tiled roof that the superbly carved cross on the attic ventilators comes to your notice. High up and non-ostentatious, it is almost possible to miss this detail altogether, making it a delightful surprise each time you catch sight of it. It is possibly my great-great-uncle—a well-to-do forest officer in colonial India who would never step out into the sweltering heat unless in his waistcoat—under whom this architectural input came about. We were in Kerala's Christian heartland, and there was the added historical pride in the community of being able to trace our lineage back to Jesus' own disciple, Saint Thomas, who had supposedly landed in Muziris in 52 AD, and baptised the first of those who would be called the Marthoma Syrian Christians.

~

I'm told this is the final day of the twenty-five-day Nativity fast, not that I knew anything about this Syrian Christian custom back then. In my twenty-seven years, never had I seen my mother, or anyone else for that matter, fast even once during this time, even though she strictly observes the forty-day Lent period before Easter every year, the only member of our family with any religious fear, and faith, in her.

Why is that so? I believe it is the occasion, the

impossibility of solemnity during Christmas, that makes all the difference. The few times I decided to observe Lent, I realised how meditative a ritual fasting—not a complete sacrifice, but abstinence from certain types of food—can be. At first a battle of will, there are moments of triumph, but as the days pass, it allows for quiet reflection of the self.

In the Christian tradition, Lent is the time in prayer that leads up to the Resurrection of Christ. The forty-day period is also synonymous with hardship, the time Christ spent in the desert, fighting the temptation of Satan—though since fasting extends over seven weeks to end with the Easter feast, it is in actuality, the anpathu noimba (fifty-day fast). Entirely voluntary, this is the fast most solemnly and sincerely observed in the community.

The Nativity fast, too, apparently used to take place over forty days, but with time it was reduced to twenty-five days, starting from the first day of December. It is meant to give thanks to God for sending his son for the salvation of his people. But during Christmas, the feasting, rather than the fasting, seems to have taken precedence. Growing up in Calcutta, my sister and I would accompany my mother to New Market two or three months beforehand for the annual purchase of dry fruits to go into her Christmas cakes. Plums, raisins, dates, orange peel and nuts. Calcutta loves its Christmas, and New Market always seemed festive during this time too, as much as Park Street and the Cathedral Church would appear in December. A busy school teacher, with two young kids and a workaholic journalist for a husband, the chopping of fruit, to be then soaked in generous portions of rum, would start well in advance, a little bit every day, with me nibbling alongside.

The cakes would be baked, and then wrapped in transparent green cellophane tied with a red bow, about a fortnight before Christmas. Even as the greeting cards started arriving by post from friends and family, to be given pride of place in the living room along with the Christmas tree, the cake exchange during family visits would start. This could even get competitive, as the quality of the cakes made by each family was analysed, the taste and texture, and whether the fruit had spread out evenly or settled in bulk at the bottom.

The Sunday before Christmas, the three of us would head to our church in Park Circus. This was no architectural wonder, but an average three-storey building in the middle of a bustling, middle-class neighbourhood. The ground floor was a busy charitable clinic run by the church; the second floor, a large, bare room used for Sunday school classes where we could escape the tedium of Malayalam church services, while the third was the home of the priest. It was the first floor that was the church itself, with seats for the congregation and, what I remember most clearly, ever-burning electric candles on both sides of the cross at the altar. The plainness of the room would transform for the evening service on Christmas Eve, as wreaths and other decorations took over the windows and walls, children performed the Nativity play and we sang along with the choir in exuberance.

We were not a family that went to church every Sunday. It is my theory that we went particularly on the Sundays that my mother, the masterful multi-tasker, wanted to buy beef at the Park Circus market. Soft undercut for beef ularthiyathu, or spicy beef fry with sliced coconut, and meat minced by hand for the beef cutlets. These would be part of the Christmas lunch, along with mutton biryani garnished with boiled eggs, a tomato-cucumber raita, fried fish, maybe meen vevichathu, a red-hot fish curry, or meen moilee, fish curry in coconut milk, and a beans thoran, stir-fried beans with grated coconut, seemingly half-heartedly thrown in for the sake of greens. That morning would have started with chicken curry and freshly-made appams, a breakfast that was reserved to make days feel special. Cake, of course, would be consumed unendingly.

That year, in Kerala, though, the food was an even more elaborately curated affair. The noimba (fasting) period meant that any celebrations, weddings or baptism, would have to wait till Christmas had passed. But with guests streaming in, a special cook was brought in, and he took over the kitchen for the next four days. Even if memories of some of the specific dishes have faded, fifteen years later, the feeling that came from eating the food remains.

~

It was a little past four in the afternoon when our bike stopped outside the gate of the ancestral property. Going up the steps, we saw the family—my parents, aunts, uncles, and my grandmother, the matriarch—watching from the porch as we crunched our way through the pebble-filled yard towards them. Helmets in hand, faces lined with soot, this was hardly a couple they could imagine walking down the aisle. Keralites—or perhaps, this is a trait of Syrian Christians—or just my family?—are not prone to great displays of physical affection, and as K with his exuberant Bengali and Punjabi upbringing watched aghast, we largely nodded or grunted through the next few minutes.

But there are little, unspoken, publicly unacknowledged ways in which I was aware these feelings are expressed. My paternal uncle, one of my father's younger brothers, an intimidating man of few words, wanted to share his love of the paper-thin pathiri and beef curry, a Kerala Muslim dish, each time we visited, and would send for it for our breakfast. There was the time he made my sister and me walk behind him downhill to the nearby river, not a word spoken in between, to his friend's house, who then took us for a ride in the narrow wooden boat.

My aunt kept gallons of kattan kaapi (black coffee) warm in a flask for her brothers to consume through the day. Ammachi, a domineering presence even at her age, would stand leaning against the edge of the dining table, peering through her cataract-filled eyes at our plates, urging us to serve ourselves more, but herself refusing to have dinner till Apppapa (my uncle) got home safe. She would remember things we had loved as children and even if our taste had changed as adults, revealing this to her would have been just hurtful.

Over the four days of that sultry winter in Kottayam, as the house filled with guests, I noticed the loud and the silent appreciation of our friends from Delhi of the Syrian Christian fare that was a routine affair for me: beef ularthiyathu, meen moilee, chicken curry, fish fry, beef cutlet, kachia moru or spiced yoghurt, iddiyappam, karimeen curry in coconut paste, thoran and avial. Sometimes, it takes an outsider's perspective to make you realise what is special about your life.

Before all this, though, was the morning after we arrived in Kottayam, Christmas itself. While my family conspired to send me to the beautician to see what could be done about my rather 'unbridely' tan, in the large old kitchen, the two firewood stoves were lit up, the heat rising up to the overhanging shelf, on which was slowly drying the mace separated from the nutmeg that grew in our backyard. Cast-iron appam chattis (pans) were placed on the fire; a fork pierced into an onion, which was dipped into the oil that would be spread evenly on the curved pans. A ladle poured the thin paste into the centre, and the chatti was given a circular spin, so that the appam's soft centre would be accompanied by a thin, crispy edge.

Chicken stew and freshly-made appam was our Christmas breakfast.

Two days of feasting later, we were married. A Delhi friend who arrived late and missed the wedding lunch was unperturbed; he'd found a bunchful of the small but richly delicious jali puvam bananas which went down his gullet in dozens.

It was time to give the bike a grateful pat on its back, and send it by train on a restful journey back home to Delhi. While the wedding party moved to Goa.

I'm Dreaming of a Goan Christmas

~ Vivek Menezes ~

*n*othing much has changed in Goa since the French adventurer François Pyrard de Laval spent the holiday season here over 400 years ago. 'All the streets are then hung with lanterns,' he writes, in the account of his escapades first published in 1611. 'On Christmas Day, in all the churches are represented the mysteries of the Nativity, with diverse characters and animals. Everyone goes to see it. Even in most of the houses and at the cross-streets they do the same; it is a prettier sight at that season there, than here (in Europe).'

Skip to 2022, and I feel exactly the same. Eager to experience Yuletide in the West over long decades of living in its greatest cities—Paris, London, New York—I wassailed and Tannenbaumed with the best of them. But all it did was to underline my conviction that the end-of-the-year holidays are unbeatably gracious and meaningful in this ancient slice of the Konkan coastline, and no one who experiences it could ever disagree. There's considerably less glitter, but who needs it when you have genuine joie de vivre? What is more, Christmas in Goa is the opposite of exclusionary. Every one of every age from every community shares the fun.

'Nobody is left out of the holiday spirit here,' says Damodar Mauzo, the beloved eminence of Goan letters and 2022 Jnanpith Award winner. Mauzo says his family participates in many aspects of the village celebrations, hanging a Christmas star in the balcao, making a crib and attending midnight mass.

The customs Mauzo describes are at the heart of Goan social culture across communities: an extensive range of painstakingly handmade delicacies, adults and children taking the time to crisscross their vaddos (village wards) to visit neighbours and friends, and exuberant creativity and craftsmanship spilling over from every household—during Ganesh Chaturthi it is the matoli (ceremonial canopy) of fruits and flowers, then the Narakasur effigy on Diwali, followed by cribs and stars in December. At Christmas, in addition to all this, there is the apex event of midnight mass, the part-solemn, part-giddy ritual of dressing up in your extravagant best, and trooping to the parish church for the long, meandering musical service that ushers in the nativity. It ends in the small hours of the 25th, but no one heads home. Instead, there are only warm embraces, lashings of coffee and slices of cake.

And here's the best bit: you too can go, everyone is welcome. What is true of the Mauzos in Majorda plays out everywhere in Goa, where the boundary walls between ostensibly different religions have been carefully kept conspicuously low, with neighbours unselfconsciously sharing the same universe of meaning in ways that can be incomprehensible to outsiders.

The acclaimed American anthropologist Robert Newman, who first visited Goa in 1965, soon after the defeat and annexation of Portugal's 451-year-old Estado da India, and proceeded to study the state for decades, writes that 'though in content the Catholic and Hindu traditions differ greatly, in form and style they have tended to move together over the past few centuries in Goa. There has emerged a specifically Goan style, which has helped forge a common Goan identity despite religious differences. This development has been more pronounced among the lower castes, but large numbers of higher-caste Hindus and Catholics also take part in certain key religious festivals, worshipping and honouring the same deities—in particular, the goddess Shantadurga and several versions of Our Lady.'

This deep-rooted syncretism permeates all aspects of Goan faith practices, and can appear surreal, even contradictory, to adherents of orthodoxy. Nonetheless, its purchase is undeniably powerful: All important feasts and festivals at every major site of worship in the state are thronged by sincere devotees of every background. Limitless co-mingling is an archetypical feature of this many-layered culture, clearly evident in music, architecture, food, and every artistic flowering.

Here, we have the salutary examples of the great Goan painters of the twentieth century, like Francis Newton Souza, the livewire modernist who kick-started Indian modernism in Mumbai in the 1940s, whose paintings of altars bristle with tantric symbology. His close contemporary, the great abstractionist Vasudeo Gaitonde—the two friends shared ancestral roots in North Goa—considered himself a non-denominational follower of St Francis of Assisi. Perhaps most illustrative is the unique bridge figure of Angelo da Fonseca, the grandee from the island of Santo Estevam, who studied at the JJ School of Art in colonial Bombay around 100 years ago but quit—and transplanted himself to Bengal—because he 'wanted to be a shishya of the best Indian artists of the time.' At the cusp of the 1930s in Santiniketan, he was the protégé of Nandalal Bose and Abanindranath Tagore, and spent the next four decades (he died in 1967) painting an astonishingly beautiful oeuvre of Indian Christian iconography that draws deep from Islamic, Hindu, Jain and Buddhist themes as well as the Western canon.

Fonseca's artworks effortlessly represent East and West simultaneously, with great harmony. They are the perfect icons for Christmas in cosmopolitan Goa, where many other conventions have evolved out of borrowings from around the world—the result of centuries of functioning as one of the earliest crucibles of globalisation. In her excellent *Cozinha De Goa: History and Tradition of Goan Food*, the historian Fátima da Silva Gracias writes vividly about the emblematic consoada (the original Portuguese word has become kuswar in Konkani), where families labour for weeks to prepare 'a plethora of sweets and savories [with] Goan, Malayan, Portuguese and Anglo-Indian recipes blended together. The Hindu "food of the gods" also has its own influence in the form of nevreo, kulkuls and shankarpalis.'

How has all this managed to make it into the twenty-first century? Perhaps it's best to consider the good news: Goans have not lost any of their gusto for Christmas, and its far-flung diaspora in every corner of the world always homes right back in at this time of the year. But there's also the less encouraging flip side: less time and more distractions have had their effect. In the past five years, there has been an immense influx of migrants and would-be settlers from other parts of India who cannot understand, refuse to participate in, and are even overtly hostile to the gentle pan-community celebrations that have characterized Goa for the past few centuries. From being communal in the best sense of the word, these kinds of feast days and festivals are being communalised in the mindless, ugly, vicious manner of our times.

So what do we do? I think it starts by savouring what survives, and working hard to save its spirit. The world now comes to Goa for Christmas, and that's perfectly okay because Christmas in Goa encompasses the world with great felicity. When my sons set up our tree at home, they adorn it with cherished reminders of family scattered on four continents, and our own travel memories from Assam to Kashmir and several countries. We listen to holiday music in Konkani, Latin, German and Spanish and reserve cult status for Run-DMC's rollicking rap classic, 'Christmas in Hollis'. But come midnight and you will find us in Fontainhas, the centrepiece of Latinate old Panjim, for midnight Mass in the street in front of the ancient St Sebastian's Chapel. You can join us too, and do linger afterwards for coffee and cake. Now *that* is really 'Joy to the World'.

Midnight Mass in the heart of Fontainhas, in the street opposite St Sebastian's Chapel.

It is traditional for most Goan houses, no matter the religion of the occupants, to hang paper stars in their windows and balconies.

Photos: Vivek Menezes

Syncretism runs very deep in Goa, where the lines between faith practices are conspicuously blurred.

The seasonal touch at the Convent of Santa Monica, still the largest in all of Asia.

Christmas decorations on the 'Holy Hill' of Old Goa.

Goa's favourite dessert is bebinca, whose recipe begins with 'Take the yolks of forty eggs...'

...and the mouth-watering bolo sans rival is where all the whites go, along with crumbled cashewnuts.

All the seasonal delicacies become consoada (kuswar), to be distributed widely among friends and family.

Gaon Ki Khushi Alag Hai

~ Mary Sushma Kindo ~

I come from Simdega Sawai—a village in the Simdega district of Jharkhand, about four hours away from Ranchi. There are twenty-five or thirty Christian families. The Christian families all live on one side of the village, and the Hindu families live on the other side. But we celebrate all the festivals together—Diwali, Holi, Christmas, Easter. There have never been any fights between the Christians and Hindus in my village. We all live together peacefully.

I don't remember when my family became Christians. Both my parents were Christian, so maybe it was in my grandparents' time, maybe before that. My parents are no more, but there are twelve or thirteen of us in my family—I have one brother and three sisters. Now, they are all married, so their children live in the village too. We do kheti-baari (farming). Even the children help in the fields when they are big enough. There is no school in my village, but there is a government school about a kilometre away, which is also for children from the neighbouring village.

There is a small church in my village but it doesn't have a service every Sunday. Only when there is some function like a wedding, then they call a padri from the big church, or if one of the Fathers is on tour and comes to our village, then he holds a service. But by church, I don't mean a 'girja'—there is no building. It is just a big verandah in a compound with trees all around, it's an open-air church. There is a grotto in the compound, with statues of Jesus and Mary, and we pray in front of the grotto.

The big church is in Sohn Pahari, which is about three or four kilometres away. This is a proper parish, with a school and a hostel and a church. There are two Fathers, and Sisters who teach in the school. They live in the hostel.

The church in Sohn Pahari is a big room with an altar, but we sit on the floor. People bring towels and chatais to sit on. There is a service every Sunday, at 7 a.m. and at 9 a.m. In winter, the services are a bit later. The service is in Hindi. Some of the Fathers who don't know Hindi speak in English, and someone translates. We sing hymns and someone plays the dholak (drum) and jhunjhun (cymbals). The boys and girls from the school and also from the neighbouring villages come and sing, and the Sisters also sing.

We all go to this church for Christmas and on Easter, and also when there is a naamkaran (christening) for someone's child. On other Sundays, two or three families from the village go to church, everyone doesn't manage to go. But on Christmas Day, we all go. Some families go at night for the service which is at 10 or 11 p.m., and some of us go in the morning. We walk to church, except for those who have motorbikes. There is no bus or public transport to Sohn Pahari, so we have to walk through the fields. Except now there are some autos in my village—big ones which can seat 10-12 people. They charge five or ten rupees per person, but only for the grown-ups, for children, it is free. But you have to book the auto in advance, because there are only two or three.

The harvesting of the crops is done before Christmas, and parents save some of the money they earn from selling the anaaj (crops) for the festival. In the village, we buy new clothes only once a year—for Christmas. All the parents buy clothes for the children, and if they can afford it, for themselves too. There is a small market near our village, or we go to the town nearby. In fact, if you ask me what I like best about Christmas—it is the new clothes that I get. It is something to look forward to the whole year!

After the service on Christmas Day, and the naach-gaana (singing and dancing), we all come home. The Fathers and Sisters don't serve any cake or chai-paani. But on that day, in every Christian home in the village, special food is made—chicken or mutton curry. On other days, we have only dal-roti and sabzi, except when special guests come—but on Christmas Day, we do have chicken or mutton. And we make namkeen and mithai at home—khajur ki roti, which is made with maida (refined flour), sooji (semolina), dates and sugar, and cheeni roti, which is made with rice. Those who can afford it buy cake from the town. And we exchange presents—mainly clothes, and toys for the children.

In the church in Sohn Pahari, the Fathers and Sisters and the boys and girls decorate the church with lights and candles and a big tree. In the village also we put up decorations in our homes, some of us get a small tree from the town. Of course, the decorations are nothing like what you see in the big markets and churches in Delhi, but everyone tries to do the best they can.

I came to Delhi when I was eight or nine years old, with some relatives who had jobs here. It is a two-day journey from my village to Delhi, and the same going back. You have to go by train to Ranchi—there is one train that leaves at 4 p.m. and reaches Ranchi around 12 noon the next day; and there is another that leaves at 8 a.m. and reaches Ranchi at 4 a.m., but quite often it gets late. From Ranchi it is a four-hour journey by bus. By the time we reach the village, it is night. There is no direct bus—we have to change on the way, and it is another hour's journey from there.

When I came to Delhi, I lived near Gol Dak Khana. My bhabhi, who was a nurse, and my brother who worked in a bank, used to teach me some reading and writing at home. I never went to school, that is why I can't read or write properly.

My father died when I was twelve or thirteen, so then I went back to the village to be with my mother. But I used to work in the fields, I didn't go to school even there. I came back to Delhi when I was eighteen or twenty, and have been here ever since, about thirty years. I got a job as a maid in a house in South Extension, and I lived with the family. I worked with them for many years till they went abroad; then I got a job with another family in Greater Kailash.

In Delhi, I have quite a few relatives who have come here to work. Here we go to church in Defence Colony—but now there is some construction going on, they are making it bigger—so we go to church in a school in Gautam Nagar. The service is very early, at 6 or 7 a.m. I would like to go every Sunday, but it is not possible. So, I only go some times, on Easter or on Christmas, if I haven't gone back to my village that year. The service is just like the one in the village, after all, most of the people are from there. Here also they play the dholak and jhunjhun but they also have a guitar and a harmonium. The hymns are a little different too, and there are three services—in Hindi, Malayalam and English.

Also, in Delhi, after the service, we get chai, coffee and cake, unlike in the village. Even so, I prefer Christmas in the village—*gaon ki khushi alag hai* (the happiness you feel in the village is different). There, we celebrate the whole week—from Christmas Eve on 24th December, the naach-gaana continues until the New Year comes. *Yesu ke gaane chalte rehte hain* (we keep singing hymns to Jesus throughout the week). Here in Delhi it is all over in one day. *Yahan pe pata bhi nahi chalta ki* Christmas *hai* (here, you don't even know that Christmas has come and gone)!

(As told in Hindi to Renuka Chatterjee)

Nativity scene in Dhanbad.

My Memories of Christmas

~ Hansda Sowvendra Shekhar ~

I grew up in Ghatsila and my earliest memories of celebrating Christmas are from school. I went to St Joseph's Convent High School in Mosaboni Mines, a school run by Catholic nuns of the Sisters of St Joseph of the Apparition Order. In fact, I learnt about Christmas and Durga Puja even before I learnt about our traditional Santhal festivals such as Baha, Karam, or Sohrai! That is, perhaps, no surprise, given how popular culture and our surroundings influence us.

In the 1980s and 90s, Durga Puja was a huge festival in Moubhandar, a small industrial township nestled quietly away from the bustle of larger places where other festivals could have had a greater following. My parents worked at the copper factory in Moubhandar and I grew up in the township. Durga Puja was *the* festival there. Holi and Diwali too used to be reasonably lavish, although they were mostly celebrated by the non-Bengali populace, with Diwali being more important for the Marwaris and those of the Baniya caste.

A procession on the occasion of Ram Navami was the norm and Chhath used to be relatively quiet and a largely private affair, but that was for those who we generalised as 'Bihari'. And there used to be a crowded mela on the banks of the river Subarnarekha on Akhan Jatra—the day after Makar Sankranti, considered to be New Year's Day on the local calendar—but that was for people who were apparently *lower* than us. It would take me more than a decade to realise and acknowledge that I too was among those people who I, in the 1980s and 90s, had considered lower than us!

The overall atmosphere in the township in those days was the genteel, Bengali one and, hence, the festival for which everyone seemed to wait for the entire year was Durga Puja. North Indian traits such as the ten-day abstinence from non-vegetarian food on the occasion of Navaratra, had not yet crept into the Durga Puja celebrations, because of which Durga Puja in those days had its Bengali—upper-class, bhadrolok Bengali, to be exact—characteristics intact. Drunk men nearly stripping themselves of all their clothes on the low-water crossway on the Subarnarekha during the visarjan (immersion) and genteel families—with women and children!—looking away as if everything was normal punctured the bubble of that gentility, but that is a story for another day. I have been told that even before I had learnt to speak properly, I had learnt to say 'puja': 'pawja', I said. I babbled to my father that he should take me to see the 'pawja', and then we went pandal-hopping.

If my fascination for Durga Puja was a result of the Bengali atmosphere in Moubhandar, my school ensured my fascination for Christmas. Mosaboni, where my school was—still is—is about 10 kms from Moubhandar. While Moubhandar is the location of the copper factory, Mosaboni is where the copper mines are. Hence, while Moubhandar was smoky and oftentimes polluted with the sulphur dioxide gas from the factory, Mosaboni was hilly and green, with more trees. My school was in a village called Mohandera just at the foot of a hill range, and during the rains and winters, and especially if it rained during the winters, my school presented a scenic view.

Christmas Day in our school was celebrated about a week before 25th December so that the school could be closed for our Christmas-cum-winter holidays by the 25th. We were told to come to school on the day of the Christmas celebration wearing what our teachers called 'colour dress'. Colour dress meant clothes that were not our school uniform.

The language of the celebration was English. Most of the nuns at our school were from south India, but I am sure there were quite a few who must have been Adivasis from places around Ranchi. I remember returning from Ranchi to Ghatsila by bus with my mother in January 1998. One of our co-passengers was a Sister from our school, and I remember that Sister telling my mother that she belonged to the Kharia Adivasi community. The services at churches these Adivasi nuns must have gone to before they joined the Order must have been conducted, I am sure, in Hindi or Sadri. The churches in Mosaboni and Moubhandar too must have conducted the services in Hindi instead of in English. Yet, in accordance with the 'only English must be spoken inside the campus' rule of our school, the language of the Christmas-cum-New Year celebrations at our school was English.

At the Christmas celebrations, there used to be songs, Santa Claus and the Christmas tree. But, more than anything else, I was amazed by those people who presented Christmas cards to the Sisters. I do not remember any Christian giving them cards. Those people—or parents, rather—who gave cards to the Sisters on the day of the Christmas-cum-New Year celebrations were usually the privileged Hindus of higher castes who held cushy jobs in the copper company. Those parents—fathers, usually—brought their children, dressed in 'colour dress', for the event, and gave cards to the Sisters and chatted with them; while the children, like children from entitled families, fussed around, hanging on to their fathers' legs even as they spoke with the Sisters. Also, they gave the Sisters these cards on the day of the celebration, that is, nearly a week before 25th December, making me wonder how and from where they managed to get their Christmas cards so early in such a small town! I did not understand several things at that age, but I did notice that *those* men were not Christians.

Where were the Christians then?

Christian students in our Christian school were usually Adivasi Christians or South Indian Christians and were quite small in number. Their parents were not officers in the copper company, nor did they hail from affluent backgrounds. The parents of one of my Tamil Christian friends were so humble that once when his mother came to meet our Principal, she took off her footwear before entering the Principal's office. Except for the husband of a Hindi teacher—who could have been either Oraon or Kharia, I am not sure—I do not remember any Adivasi Christian man who was both an officer in the copper company and also had a direct connection with my school. It is not too hard to understand now why the actual Christians were invisible at the Christmas celebration at an English-medium Christian convent school: basically, an elite place.

Yet, in those days of innocence, Christmas fascinated me. I got my parents to buy me a Christmas star with a small light bulb inserted inside it. I still remember the colour of that star: shiny red. We hung that star in the veranda of our bungalow, glowing beautifully for several nights till my Christmas fever for that season wore off.

For quite some time, people in my school believed that I was a Christian. I think that was because, in those days, it was taken for granted that any educated Adivasi family in a position of privilege had to be Christian. In those days, non-Adivasis perhaps found it difficult to believe that non-Christian Adivasis with no exposure to education and opportunities provided by Christian missionaries too were capable of procuring an education on their own. I knew we were not Christians; yet, just to double-check, I came home and asked my father, 'Are we Christians?' My father decided to play along, so he laughed and told me, 'Tell them we're from the Chhota church.'

The Chhota or Small Church is the Protestant Church, as opposed to the Bada or Big Church which is the Roman Catholic Church. My father put me in the Small Church because he thought my Roman Catholic Sisters would start looking for me in their Big Church. Sometime later, though, my father decided that the joke had gone on for long enough and started taking me to jaher, the sacred grove of us Santhals, to inform me that we were animist Adivasis and not Christians.

The highlight of my Christmas celebrations was when, in the winter of 1992, I was chosen to play Santa Claus at the Christmas-cum-Annual Night function of our school. Of all the students in our school, I was chosen to play that part. My entry was at the end of the function, dancing along from the back of the hall to the front to a version of 'Jingle Bells', throwing toffees at the audience and shaking hands with the guests.

Christmas in Ghatsila, though a major festival, is a relatively quiet affair. In Moubhandar, there are two churches: St Anthony's Catholic Church, and the Anglican Protestant Church which was established in 1946. During Christmas, both these church buildings are beautifully decorated with colourful lights, and Christmas songs in Sadri and Hindi are played. I remember one Hindi song, *Paida hua hai taaranhaara/Dekho, charni mein leta hua* (The Saviour is born/He is lying in the manger), and a Sadri song, *Charni ka tara tim-tim-tim-tim chamkela* (The star in the manger twinkles). In Ghatsila, there is a Grace Union Church in Kashida, but I have not seen it during Christmas time yet.

Christmas brings back memories of cakes, rose cakes and arsa pitha. Most of the nurses in the hospital where my mother worked were Christian Adivasis. After returning from their respective churches on the morning of 25th December, they sent us tiffin boxes full of Christmas goodies they had made at home. These goodies could also be found at the iconic ICC Bakery in Mosaboni, just opposite St Barbara's Catholic Church which opened in 1968. The oldest bakery in Ghatsila, it has been around since before Independence—when sahebs used to run the copper company—and their baked items are famous. A little away from ICC Bakery in Mosaboni is the oldest Grace Union Church, established as early as in 1939. On the road between Moubhandar and Mosaboni, at a place called Surda Mines, I used to eagerly peer out of the school bus to spot the cute little building of the Emmanuel Tamil Church. Churches are important markers in history. It would be interesting to learn why, in this area, Protestant churches are older than Catholic churches.

Ghatsila has always been a popular tourist destination, especially among the Bengalis from Kolkata who have to, as if setting off on a pilgrimage, visit the house where the well-known writer Bibhutibhushan Bandopadhyay had lived and died. Subarnarekha River bank, Burudih Dam, Dharagiri Falls, Galudih barrage, Purnapani and the Rankini Mandir in Jadugora are other popular picnic spots around Ghatsila, which visitors throng during the Christmas-New Year season.

I worked for five years in Pakur, and Christmas in Pakur is as quiet as in Ghatsila. The Bengali Methodist Church—a huge and impressive red building—and the Jidato Mission campus surrounding this church need to be seen. They are as beautiful as any tourist spot. Popular picnic spots and places worth visiting in and around Pakur include Sido-Kanhu Park, Dharni Pahar, Prakriti Vihar in Amrapara, St Luke's Mission campus in Hiranpur, the hot water springs in Maheshpur, Motijharna Falls in Sahebganj, Massanjore Dam in Dumka and the Hazaarduaari Palace in Murshidabad.

Now I work and live in Chandil, home to the Chandil Dam on the Subarnarekha River and the Dalma Wildlife Sanctuary. There is a United Missionary Church in Chandil which I often pass by as it is quite close to the block office, but I have not been able to see it at Christmas time. In December 2019, an Oraon nurse of our health centre gave me a gift on Christmas: a lovely and immensely useful messenger bag made of red tartan cloth from the shop run by the Indian Society for Promoting Christian

Knowledge (ISPCK) at Bahu Bazar in Ranchi. An ISPCK calendar card for the year 2020 accompanied that bag and I taped the calendar on the door of my pad in Chandil. I have not been able to take that calendar off the door because I have this tendency to leave things where they are, undisturbed. Every time I look at that calendar, I wonder how things have changed after 2020!

I have only heard about Christmas in Ranchi and Jamshedpur, not experienced those yet. I am especially impressed by their church buildings. However, I am no longer enamoured by festivals, not even my own. Nowadays, I only wish for an entire day to sleep without being disturbed, and uneventful and injury-free festival days and nights.

In Search of an East Indian Christmas in Mumbai

~ Deborah Rosario ~

I spent seven years in the UK and thoroughly revelled in the annual Christmas festivity there. The whole country united in celebrating, whether it was tinkling Christmas carol tunes in shops or the ubiquity of mulled wine and mince pies at social gatherings. I was based in Oxford and the choral music at college chapels was glorious and uplifting. There was even the chance that, if there was snow, we would see a white Christmas.

It may seem odd to introduce a piece on Indian Christmases with my recollections of Christmas in the UK, but my British experience threw my Indian Christmas into stark relief. It helped me rediscover what was Indian about my Christmas. When I returned, there were certain elements of a UK Christmas that I tried to recapture. But I also pursued the quest for an Indian Christmas.

My father is Goan and my mother is East Indian. East Indians are a Christian community, based in Mumbai, called so because they were close to the East India Company. Over time, our family connections to the Goan side of our family all but evaporated as many relatives relocated to Portugal. My East Indian ties, however, have only thickened throughout my life, and therefore it was an East Indian Christmas that I was seeking. Instead of seeking the Christmas fairy tale of a European idyll, I sought the Christmas colour and climate, metaphorically speaking, that only my specific locality could bring to life.

One, main, contrast between the UK and Mumbai is the weather. Unlike the UK's cold weather, temperate weather prevails in a Mumbai December. Temperatures go down from the high 30s to the 20s, and if we are lucky, further down to a minimum of 17 or 18 degrees Celsius. We do not wear heavy woollens but, nevertheless, the weather is an excuse to liberate our light jackets and sweaters from our closets. On trains, in the early mornings, one might even see individuals bundled up in thick socks and scarves, something that the mild weather hardly warrants.

Another contrast between the UK and India that caught my attention is that since India is not even a nominally Christian nation like the UK, Christmas celebrations do not permeate the entire country in quite the same way. Members of other communities increasingly conduct some token celebration of Christmas, perhaps decorating a tree or wearing a Santa hat. But to experience a true community-wide celebration of Christmas, you must tour a location peopled with Christian residents.

It is for this reason that during the weeks leading to Christmas, I drive around the by-lanes of Bandra. It is rather wonderful to turn the corner from a non-celebrating district and come upon, like a revelation, celebratory Bandra scenes. This historically Christian suburb truly radiates Christmas. I drive around the winding streets and allow myself to be infected by the Christmas spirit that is a tangible thing in the air. Bungalows and streetlamps are wreathed with Christmas lights. Christmas music wafts out of houses. Shops and street-side stalls run by women sell colourful Christmas sweets. The streets are alive with a carnivalesque atmosphere, thronged with purposeful shoppers intent on acquiring festive goods. Hill Road is a-shimmer with the tinsel of Christmas decorations on sale.

Indeed, decorating the home is a central part of Christmas traditions. Come December, we dust off the decorations that have been tucked away in storage. While countries like the UK usually install full-size, even real trees, Indian Christmases use artificial trees, and what we have found most convenient is the three-foot Christmas tree, no less precious for its size, that suits our small flat. We set it up on a low side-table along with miniature ornaments and additional flourishes of greenery.

Perhaps one of the most extensive exertions at Christmas time is the making of sweets, another contrast to the UK. UK's sweets are all awash in the colours of brown and burgundy—their dusky Christmas cakes, mince pies and mulled wine, for instance. Indian Christmas sweets of East Indian traditions, by contrast, pop with variegated shapes and colours. Milk cream might be pale, but marzipan typically melds two or three colours in each piece. Both are moulded into flowers, angels, and other intricate shapes. Jujubes are cubes of brightly jewelled colours dusted with sugar. There are coconut tartlets in multiple colours, rose-hued cashew sweet, claret-coloured guava cheese, pastel green soji sweet and more.

During my childhood years, my mother would spend the evenings in the weeks before Christmas carefully cooking sweets. She had to spend hours at the stove, painstakingly stirring the mixture, and stay vigilant to prevent it from overcooking. It had to reach just the right consistency. For marzipan and milk cream, one has to drop the batter in cold water and see if it can be moulded in one's hands. For jujubes, the batter must drip from a spoon and display a 'two-thread' consistency.

As children, my brother and I would take particular delight in milk cream and marzipan which we would spend almost entire nights moulding. We had to judiciously eyeball the size of the mould we were using and estimate the amount of dough we needed. We would daintily pluck out small amounts from the cream-, pink- and green-coloured dough and roll them into a cohesive ball in the palm of our hands. Then we would gently press the dough into the mould. After filling up a tray of moulds, we would turn them upside-down and, with gentle but decisive taps, dislodge the sweets. The trick was in extracting them whole with smooth edges.

I enjoy these Indian elements to Christmas, but Christmas in Mumbai has also been internationalised. After returning from the UK, I have found many of the continental treats I loved there available at our local bakeries. While Theobroma serves some of these, I enjoy soaking up the Christmas atmosphere at the elaborately decorated American Express bakery in Bandra. I stock up on mince pies, stollen and Christmas pudding. Over time, I have come to conclude that this penchant for British ways is not necessarily extraneous to my family traditions. East Indians always had an affinity for the British and drew on their customs. Blending English and Indian elements—the 'chutnification' of English elements, the anglicization of Indian elements—were always part of our traditions.

These days, the pace of life is too rapid for us to home-make our own sweets, so we order them from a relative who caters these. But I do still labour over my own Christmas cake. The East Indian Christmas cake is a white one speckled with glints of red and green fruit peel. I also make the English Christmas cake that is a rich brown and whose batter is mixed with dry fruit and rum or whiskey.

We also participate in the long-standing practice of

distributing trays of sweets. When I was a child, there would be an exchange of sweets with other Christian neighbours, family and friends. We would assemble trays of an assortment of the sweets we had made and give them away in exchange for other families' home-made treats. This often led to the scrupulous evaluation and comparison of sweets by all the aunties involved: This one had achieved just the right shade of pale ivory. This one was made with cashew rather than almond. That one had too much rose essence. The colours were much too dark in the other one.

These days, we live in a cosmopolitan suburb of Mumbai, Andheri (West), and have lost these close connections to a tightly-knit Christian community. We do distribute trays to a few neighbours of both Christian and other faiths. In return, we receive sweets from one or two Christian families at Christmas time, and from other families at the time of their festivals.

Besides sweets, Christmas would not be Christmas without music. My Protestant church organises a variation on neighbourhood carolling in the weeks before Christmas. The church choir visits and serenades different members of the congregation who volunteer for this, and others may also attend. Carols are interspersed with Christmas readings from the Bible, akin to a 'Nine Carols and Lessons' service in the British tradition. We usually turn out all electric lights and light wax candles for the singing of 'Silent Night', before we conclude with a joyous ringing out of 'Feliz Navidad'. The hosting family serves refreshments at the conclusion, and we all enjoy a time of congenial fellowship together.

There are also concerts at the National Centre for Performing Arts (NCPA) where I can catch a medley of carols. These are not the medieval and early modern carols that I often heard in Oxford. Rather, the favourites here are nineteenth-century and mid-twentieth-century classics with a few contemporary and home-crafted carols thrown in for good measure.

Christmas Day celebrations have varied over the years. But when I travel back to Christmases growing up, I return to a more traditional Christmas and a more communal one.

These traditional Christmases have roots even further back in time, and I learned of them from my mother's memories of growing up in the middle decades of the twentieth century. I can trace back parent traditions as well as those that are almost completely alien to the times we know.

~

In those days, one of the first tasks that claimed attention during the Christmas season was what has now become the lost art of writing cards. Hill Road then surged, not with decorations and sweets which were usually homemade, but with Christmas cards. It was a well-worn practice to make Christmas card lists and dispatch cards to family and friends, at home and abroad. Rather than opting for the anonymity of buying cards in bulk, my mother's family would attend to each individual on the list singly, selecting a card to suit each one. The cards were handwritten during a night-time vigil at the dining table. A sharp eye was kept on the calendar to ensure that the cards reached their recipients in time. Much thought was also given to the post office visit. This was plotted for a time when the queues would be navigable.

Then came the scouring of the house. The family effected a thorough purge of dust. The method of choice for the washing of floors was a deluge of water and scrubbing with washing soda. Around this time, all the houses in the area emanated a clean freshly-washed smell, and the lanes ran over with rivulets of water draining out of the houses. New curtains replaced old ones. Christmas decorations were rarely purchased but were cleverly constructed at home. Assorted baubles, holly leaves, berries and the like, were put together with thermacol and cellophane paper. Christmas trees were in fact a rare sight, but colourful streamers lined the walls. Christmas cards received from relatives and friends were also strung across the walls like bunting. A crib was the centrepiece of decorations in most homes. In my mother's home, wheat was grown in used food tins in the weeks prior to Christmas and stood near the crib to represent grass. Fluffy white balls of cotton might represent snow. Christmas carols could be heard through windows, streaming from radios and gramophones.

Another Christmas preparation was getting your

clothes ready. Ready-mades were not common in those days. Instead, families had their clothes stitched by a local tailor. My mother's family would browse through pattern books months ahead. A foreign pattern book like *Woman and Home* was highly prized by the ladies. The family would bookmark patterns for Christmas, and materials were purchased from Crawford market where a well-known shop offered fine fabrics for Catholic feast days and weddings. Like planning the calendar for cards, it was important to reserve your place with the tailor well in advance so that your dress was ready for Christmas.

A cornerstone of Christmas preparation was obviously the planning and making of foods and sweets. One or two families in each of Mumbai's East Indian villages would rear a pig for Christmas feasting. Near Christmas, the squeal of the pig would resound as it was beheaded and prepared for dishes like vindaloo and sorpotel. Today, we might flinch at the sound, but in those days, residents were inured to these happenings which were part of the fabric of life.

My mother's family would similarly order a roast suckling for Christmas. The evening before was occupied in chopping up and preparing the stuffing. This was inserted into the pigling the morning of Christmas Day and sent over with a help called Matthias on a thaal, a large steel plate, covered with newspaper, to the local marketplace oven where it was baked along with other families' thaals. That afternoon, the pigling would be returned, its newspaper cover drenched in oil. The rich aromas of baked pigling and the sound of sizzling skin would permeate the air. A general rush to the kitchen would ensue—to snap off and crunch on pieces of crisp skin in advance of the meal.

Vindaloo and sorpotel were prepared in the days ahead of Christmas. Since they were soaking in vinegar, which preserved the meat, they were stored outside the fridge in ceramic jars in the cool winter weather. My grandmother and some ladies of the family would sit on low, flat wooden stools around a kerosene stove, away from the regular stove on the counter-top, and fry fugias. East Indian sausages were also prepared. Like Goan sausages, meat is chopped but mixed with East Indian masalas, stuffed into the gut of an animal, and then finally apportioned into segments by tying sections off with a string.

No one bought sweets but every home made their own in the weeks preceding Christmas. Families produced a wide array of sweets. My mother's family made milk cream, marzipan, nankhatais, kulkuls, neories, coconut sweet and others. My grandmother cooked sweets on the kerosene stove whose flame could be turned low. Christmas cake was prepared at night and sent to the local oven for baking in the morning. The day before Christmas, trays of sweets would be distributed among the neighbours. Unlike now, when we employ disposable paper plates with paper napkins, my mother's family used glass plates or china and cloth napkins for this purpose. Plates received were filled up with the family's sweets and returned. It was common to compare and list the number of sweets you had made that year.

And what happened on Christmas Day? Religious observances signalled the start of things. My mother's family was Catholic, and events began with Confession the evening before. As we have seen, much of Christmas was about planning your time and minding queue lengths. Here too, someone would inform you of when the queue was short, and you would rush to church to get Confession done. The next day, the family would be up early in the morning for mass. But it was important to be back at the house in time for Santa Claus who would swagger through the neighbourhood with his troupe, chortling and calling out 'Ho! Ho! Ho!' and 'Merry Christmas'. This was organised by St Vincent De Paul, a charity which ministers to the poor and elderly. There was much hysteria over greeting Santa. The family would gather to see Santa pass the back door and then run to the front door to follow his journey through the village with their eyes.

After church, the family would have tea and a piece of Christmas cake. Then came hot soup for the cold winter morning. My grandmother would organise a tureen of soup with small tender pieces of chicken, a calde of chicken soup.

Before lunch, the elders of the family would sip on the local hooch and feni, home-brewed alcohol. My grandmother used to make a mulled hooch, warmed with brown sugar and spices. Even the smallest children were served a peg. Then the various family members ceremoniously apologised to each other for wrongs committed through the past year. This would ironically give rise to fights as old quarrels were resurrected. But someone would come along and soothe raw feelings, for, after all, it was Christmas.

At lunch, everyone sat down at the long dining table. My grandmother and great-aunt apparently never sat down with the rest of the family because they were continuously preoccupied with serving. Besides the aforesaid roast suckling, vindaloo, sorpotel, sausages, and fugias, the table would also be laden with khudi curry (made with bottle masala and ground coconut) or some other chicken curry, and pea pulao, a rice preparation.

During the afternoon, everyone napped. In the evening, tea and Christmas cake was served again. Later, when my mother was a young adult, the young folk would convene at my mother's house attired in suits and dresses, and then make their way to the Bandra Gymkhana for the Christmas dance.

Even more so than today, one felt that the whole Bandra community exuded Christmas. Houses and streets were illuminated, the smell of traditional dishes and sweets permeated the air and people greeted each other in the streets.

~

Delving into the history of our traditions reminds me of why Christmas remains a highlight of any year. We know that Christmas is not celebrated in the season of the calendar in which the historic event likely took place. Secondly, there is in fact no Biblical injunction to celebrate Christmas (though there is one to remember Jesus's death). Nevertheless, the myriad traditions that layer over the day make Christmas the most resonant of Christian feast days.

Christmas is held on just one day, but its traditions build up a sense of anticipation that extends the holiday to a whole season. Commemorative traditions burnish the season and the day so that it stands out as both hallowed and celebratory. Further, when we participate in Christmas traditions, we stand in unison with a chorus of voices, composed of local communities, the global church, and Christian communities down history who have celebrated this day.

And what better way to honour that mysterious and profound event, the incarnation, the entry of the divine into human space and time, the accommodation of the divine in the human body, the identification of the divine with human trials and felicities! It is this message of Christmas, Immanuel—God—is with us, that is at the heart of Christmas, and that I commemorate with reverence and joy.

NUESTRA SEÑORA DEL ROSARIO
(Angela Trindade. Arte religioso indígena.)
S. M. 35   Con aprob. ecca.

Card with a reproduction of 'Our Lady of the Rosary',
a painting by the Mumbai-born Goan artist
Angela Trindade.

Bombay Blues and Ghosts

~ Jane Borges ~

Of the thirty-four Christmases I have celebrated, fifteen were in Muscat, the home of my childhood. The remaining in Bombay, a city after my own heart.

My family moved back from the Gulf in 2003, a time of great change and uncertainty in my own life. Sixteen as I was—fighting obesity, hormones and the vacuum that came with the loss of old friends—there was also so much newness to embrace. I had coloured my hair (for the first and last time), got my eyebrows done, put myself through the pain of a full-body wax, shed 15 kilos (the magic of Mumbai's air), and enrolled at the illustrious St Xavier's College in Mumbai.

It was a beautiful mess.

Nearly six years earlier, in 1997, my parents had bought a quaint home in a Catholic pocket in South Mumbai—the neighbourhood of Cavel that I would end up eulogising in my debut novel, *Bombay Balchão*, several decades on. Like most middle-class families that hesitated to take bank loans, my parents chose to pour their life-savings as initial instalments for the home, selling a flat in far-flung Vasai, a sleepy cousin of Mumbai, and borrowing from relatives, to pay up for the rest.

When we arrived in Mumbai, dad was still saving up so that he could be debt-free. He had quit his job in Muscat, a move that had raised eyeballs. Admittedly, he did not have a plan. In hindsight, it would have been great if he had one, but that would make the lived experiences of our family very different. And to be honest, I would not trade that life for anything else in the world.

The shift was tough, and the financial constraints did not make it any easier on us. Christmas of 2003 was going to be a humble affair. A few traditions continued nonetheless. Like the making of sweets. Our family has roots in Karnataka and Goa, and the sweets reflect the best of both these worlds. I vaguely remember my parents going to the nearby Crawford Market, and picking up bagsful of maida, self-rising flour, semolina, dry fruits, butter, cocoa powder and sugar from Lobos, the kirana store, where all of Bombay visits to shop before Christmas. The flour would be kneaded, the butter melted and cocoa mixed with rum, soaked raisins and nuts, to make the delicious kuswar platter (a plate of traditional treats comprising neureos, kalkals, chakris, doce, guava cheese, marzipan and rum cake). My mum is also a genius winemaker. A month before Christmas, she starts working her magic with grapes, orange, pineapple, and ginger. That year, she only fermented grapes.

We spent the next few days unpacking our Christmas boxes, putting together remnants of the life we had left behind, into the new one we were building, brick by brick. The seven-foot-long tree was the first to come up. Its branches fanned out wide enough, leaving little room to walk in and out of the door adjacent to it. Dad opened the plastic tubs brimming with tiny Christmas ornaments, bubble-wrapped to prevent breakage. We sat around him, in a little circle, carefully hanging one ornament at a time, recalling stories about how we had found them on our tree—the big Santa head that we picked up from a fancy mall, the many candy canes of which we had a set of twenty, the glittery baubles that a late friend had gifted us, and the golden star dad had bought the year my youngest brother was born.

Muscat was no longer home...it had become a story. Moving countries can be emotionally crushing. For me and my brothers, Muscat was the only place we had ever known. For my parents, it was the city that helped redeem them from the inadequacies of their middle-class lives in Bombay. We were all back now, reclaiming a past that was still a part of us.

A sweet memory from that Christmas season was the carollers, guitar and tambourine in tow, who visited our building compound and belted out carols. It was my first time in a predominantly Goan Catholic neighbourhood. Back in Muscat, our immediate neighbours were Pakistanis, Sri Lankans and Bangladeshis, so our idea of belonging came from shared food, cricket and Bollywood. Here, surrounded by the Colacos, D'Costas, D'Souzas, Duckworths and Chaves, I was becoming fully aware of my Catholic identity.

On Christmas Eve, the star was lit, as was the tree. Jim Reeves' 'Christmas Songs' played on my dad's music system. As we left home to attend midnight mass in church, which was on the same road as our home, my father slid the figurine of Baby Jesus, the hero of our Christmas crib, into his breast pocket. When we returned two hours later, he promptly placed Baby Jesus where it belonged, snugly between the figurines of Joseph and Mother Mary.

The family was complete. Christmas was here.

I remember my brothers rushing to the tree soon after. Dad had always played Santa Claus, hiding gifts under the tree. There were none this time around. 'Santa has probably lost his way,' my father said, trying to pacify them. He hated lying, I knew.

The next day went by softly. We have no Christmas photographs from that year, but if my memory serves me right, a few relatives did come over for lunch. The evening was quieter.

Jim Reeves continued to haunt us in his smooth baritone:

I'll have a blue Christmas without you
I'll be so blue thinking about you
Decorations of red on a green Christmas tree
Won't mean a thing, dear, if you're not here with me.

The thing about Christmas is that it comes and goes so swiftly—like a cold draught that whizzes past you when you open the window on a wintry morning—that it is impossible not to leave you feeling dejected. That day, more so, it hit me like a ton of bricks.

I was missing Muscat. I missed how busy our home would have been through Christmas Day, with friends trickling in just to feast on my mum's neureos and wine, and steamed sannas, slathering it with pork curry, chattering away, telling us how they will come again, next Christmas, and every other Christmas so that we could all celebrate together. I missed how alive my home would feel. I also missed the gifts.

In Mumbai, we slowly learned to make new meaning of this day. Some years later, my brother and I joined a Christmas choir called Singspirators, which sang from one church to another all through December, spreading the cheer that we grew up believing in. My mother, the kindred spirit that she is, still revels in her love for feeding, sharing Christmas sweets each year in the neighbourhood. My father recently found a new red star to replace the gold one—it shines just as bright when lit up in the warm glow of the incandescent bulb—and happier Christmas songs, to play along with his favourite Reeves.

These new experiences now form a part of our collective muscle memory—they have taught us how to negotiate through what we had, and what we have. We have lost many family members and friends in these intervening years, but in coming to terms with the inevitability of an end—that of time, place and people— we have also realised that there are still days when we can celebrate whatever little we continue to have. Thank God for Christmas!

~

I was once ghosted on the dance floor of a Christmas Ball. I don't know why exactly I am sharing this trivia, except so you know how I landed at the ball in the first place.

In Mumbai, there are as many kinds of Christmases as there are Christians. The devout and religious usually prefer a solemn celebration: midnight mass on Christmas Eve, followed by a prayer service the next morning and perhaps, one last rosary before hitting the sack. The blithe make merry on free-flowing booze and the festive spread of roasted turkey, chicken xacuti, cafreal and sorpotel. The more conservative enjoy quietly in the comforts of their home, with an unshowy get-together. And then there are the 'gymkhana-goers' who see wisdom in song and dance.

The gymkhanas are community clubs, oddly named

to mean 'gym or sports arenas', when in reality, they are everything but that. They function like a social centre where you catch up with friends for a meal or drink, enjoy a games and dance night, or celebrate other grander events of life. All at a premium, of course. Membership fees can come at the price of a liver, kidney or any other precious body organ. Not to mention, there is a rigorous vetting process before you are made a member. The Christians have a handful of these across the city—at the top of my hat, I can think of the Catholic, Khar and Bandra gymkhanas. There could be more, but this is not a history lesson.

Every year, a grand ball—a gift of our colonial hangover—is organised at these venues on Christmas Day. Clothes are bought specifically for this occasion. Men are only allowed entry in suits—a neck or bow tie could be a sweet addition. And women: strictly dresses—good news, you get to determine its length, width and how much you would like the neckline to plunge.

I have never been a member of the gymkhana, nor has my family. Even if my parents could afford one, they always found better use for their money. It is why, for the longest time, the Christmas dance eluded me. I was disappointed of course, but hopeful.

And then one day, in the Bombay winter of 2015, my neighbour, a member at the Catholic Gymkhana at Marine Drive, telephoned. She had a spare couple pass on her, and mentioned that her friend, this dashing young man, was wondering if I could accompany him for the dance.

Here was my chance finally.

The day arrived, and so did I. But where was my dance partner?

8 p.m. On his way.
9 p.m. No sign of him yet.
10 p.m. Phone number unavailable.
11 p.m. Phone switched off.

After keeping me on tenterhooks for over three hours, I resigned myself to my fate. He was not coming. 'He may have got cold feet,' my friend said, apologetically.

I gave him the benefit of doubt, of course. He could have overslept after attending back-to-back Christmas prayer services. Who knows?

But there I was at my first gymkhana dance, albeit alone. Wait, not for too long.

Did I forget to mention that I ran into my eight-year-old nephew at the party? He was as surprised to see me as I was to meet him. The little kid had joined his parents, my cousin and his wife, who were enjoying the festivities like any adult would. A little lost—the two of us—in this surreal milieu, we made the unspoken pact of sticking together. A teetotaller then, it was easy for me to settle for an orange juice with him, while filling up our plates with chutney sandwiches, mince cutlets, kebabs and chicken lollipops. The night was still young, so we danced a bit, rather clumsily. He taught me to twist and do salsa in return for a short jive demo.

The celebrations picked up post-midnight, with guests arriving fashionably late, as they are wont to.

Everyone was dressed to the nines, all wanting to make an impression that would last them until the Christmas dance next year.

Ribbons of gossip filtered from one table to the other, when the most stunning or notorious passed by. The sometimes jarring, but mostly canorous sounds from the four-member live band whisked the air, fanning this jamboree, and forcing even the drunk to give up their glasses for a while and brave a dance on the floor. At some point, my nephew was too sleepy to keep up with the shenanigans, and slumped languidly into a chair. Bored as I was, I joined him, and played spectator instead.

The show went on, as the sexy waltzers slowly made way for the acrobatic jivers, before the wilder broke into hip hop and pop, and the rowdier took to the Goan masala—no, it is not food, but a medley of crazy, popular Konkani tracks that Catholic celebrations in Mumbai (and Goa) just cannot do without. The crowd was in a tizzy. Most people had come here with their partners, but on the dance floor, there were no rules. A few pairs of eyes hopelessly darted through the crowd vying for someone else's attention, some soaked in the lingering glances of their admirers, while others clutched on to their gorgeous partners for dear life, lest they slip. Before dawn, hands were swapped, new friends were made and phone numbers exchanged… some would call, many would not. Expectations were already being set, and romances had begun to bloom.

When I left at 4 a.m., the tables bore half-full glasses of whisky, wine and beer that had traversed the most that night, from the bar and back, and once again to the bar. I remembered telling myself right then that while this was a very merry celebration, it was not my kind of Christmas. Let us just take a moment to thank the 'ghoster' for enabling such clarity.

Did Your First Christmas Cake Come Out of an Ammunition Box Too?

~ Easterine Kire ~

When we were small, our mothers baked our birthday cakes themselves. They also baked all the Christmas cakes for the house. There was nothing very unusual about that. However, in the 1950s and '60s, they may have been the only mothers doing their baking in ammunition boxes left behind by British troops. Mother tells me that all the girls who were members of the Worldwide Guild were taught cake-baking by the missionary Tanquist's wife.

After the War, the cake baking course was taught both to students and their older siblings who had dropped out of school. The baking students included my mother and her friends. The course was multi-pronged. The girls learned to speak English after the baking; they were also taught English songs. At the end of every lesson, they always stood in a circle and said something called a 'sentence prayer' where everyone in the circle had to pray one sentence in English. Not everyone managed to pray when their turn came. However, they all learned to bake cakes and as the years passed, this tradition was handed down from generation to generation, from mother to daughter and from daughter to granddaughter.

Mrs Tanquist baked her cakes in a big mud oven, but her students ingeniously used ammunition boxes after the men discovered they were airtight and preserved heat very well.

I remember our family's ammunition-box oven very well. It was a heavy rectangular box, and it fit very well over our wood fire. But the heat regulator did not come with the box, as the Brits probably never imagined it would be used for such an activity after the boxes had served their primary purpose. So, the baker had to sit by the wood fire, constantly stoking it and eventually reducing the fire to embers when a good half hour or twenty minutes had passed. Mother says they always timed the cake. If an overeager baker opened the door during the baking process, the rising cake would fall flat on its face. I can still hear Mother admonishing us, 'Don't you open the door yet!' as we sat impatiently on cold winter nights waiting for our cakes to be done.

In our family, special evenings were reserved for

cake baking because it involved so much labour. First, Mother would mix the flour, eggs, melted butter, sugar and baking powder in a bowl and a burly male relative would be put to work to stir the batter. She strictly insisted that the batter be stirred clockwise. Naturally the batter-stirrer would slow down after some time. When that happened, we happily took over. But our little arms quickly tired from the exercise. It would take at least an hour of stirring batter to get a consistency that was smooth enough to satisfy Mother.

While the stirrers were busy, the others would be lining cake tins with buttered paper. My elder sister usually took charge of the preparation, cutting up white paper with precision into the exact shapes of the cake tins. Once the batter was ready, it was carefully poured into the tins which went into the heated ammunition box and the waiting would begin. Looking back, I see that the labour created good bonding as the whole family participated in it together.

One Christmas, my best friend and I decided we would bake a cake. When the batter was ready, I expected her mother to bring out their family's ammunition box and put it on the fire. To my surprise, they filled a big pot with sand and warmed the sand on the fire. When the sand became very hot, we were taught to make tin-sized depressions in it, and place our cake tins in them. The baking took less than an hour. Our cakes were soon ready. The advantage of the sand-layered pot was that the sand prevented the cakes from getting burned. With the ammunition boxes, the one problem that we never managed to correct was that the cakes would burn quite quickly if not taken out precisely in time. Back then, it never occurred to us to write to the British army and ask if they could correct this design flaw. And now, forty years later, it has become irrelevant since electric ovens can be bought from the Army Canteen or from the departmental stores.

I count it a great privilege to have grown up in a period when mothers made such ingenious use of abandoned ammunition boxes. I shall tell my grandchildren with great relish of the good old days when Christmas cakes tasted way better because they were made with love and watchfulness and applied creativity.

Santa Comes in a Rickshaw

The Bow Barracks Story

~ Nazes Afroz ~

Come December, the residents of Bow Barracks in central Kolkata take out their dancing shoes as the preparations for Christmas celebrations begin. What used to be intimate family gatherings or Christmas balls in community halls, has turned into a full-fledged street carnival over the past two decades, and everyone is welcome. Newspaper and local television reports as well as photos and videos shared on social media have put a sudden spotlight on the 'Christmas street party' of Bow Barracks. Kolkata's Bengali and non-Bengali revellers now throng the street, lined by two rows of red-brick terrace

apartment buildings, to witness the music and dance and to buy the home-brewed sweet wine and Christmas cake that some of the Anglo-Indian families residing there make.

Bow Barracks was built to house the Allied forces stationed in Kolkata during the Great War between 1914 and 1918. When the troops left at the end of the War, the buildings were handed over to the Calcutta Improvement Trust that in turn rented them out to the city's Christian families, mostly Anglo-Indians. A few Chinese-Indian and other Christian families too were allocated apartments there. Since then, Bow Barracks has remained an important signpost of the Christians in Kolkata.

Kolkata's encounter with Christianity goes back to the time of its foundation. More than three centuries ago, three small villages on the east bank of the Hooghly River were transformed into the modern trading post and city of Calcutta, as it was then called, by the British East India Company. The Company's trading post soon became the capital of India and the second-most important city in the British Empire. Other Europeans such as the French, the Portuguese, the Dutch, the Danes and the Greeks also landed in the city for trading and to acquire a slice of the fortune that the rich lands of Bengal were offering. Their presence was marked by the building of churches of various orders and European denominations in and around Calcutta. So, it is not surprising that Christmas celebrations have been an important part of the city's cultural landscape. The Christmas luncheon and the ball dance at the residence of the Governor General of the Company became fabled. Such grandeur continued after the British monarchy took over the rule of India from the

Company. The new rich classes of Calcutta that benefitted from the British colonial project soon began to ape European culture and lifestyles, and by the late 1800s, they had become regulars at the Christmas merriment at high-end restaurants and hotels like Firpo's and the Great Eastern.

Gradually, the Bengali middle-class, too, was having its taste of Christmas in the form of locally made cheap cakes wrapped in red cellophane paper or covered with ultra-sugary frosting. But they were never part of the revelry of the 'saheb para', as the European part of the city was called. The 'saheb para' was more than a geographical area; it was a concept—a mental state with which the emerging Bengali middle class could not identify but secretly aspired to attain.

When the Europeans left the city after India became independent, the onus of Christmas celebrations in Kolkata was passed on to the Anglo-Indians, the mixed-race community of Indian and English parentage. And the music- and dance-loving Anglo-Indians have transformed the city's Christmas festivities, making them democratic, public and entirely unique.

Grotto of Virgin Mary at the entrance of Bow Barracks.

Photos: Nazes Afroz

A Bow Barracks family waits for the street party to begin.

Onlookers view the street party from their balcony.

Generations exchange stories as the party gets going.

Santa Claus arrives at the central road of Bow Barracks in a hand-pulled rickshaw.

Dancing begins as the music opens.

The tempo of music and dance picks up as more people join the party.

A local talent croons for the revellers.

On the evening after Christmas, the bingo party for the seniors in Bow Barracks gets underway beneath the stars.

Christmas in the Moon Place

~ Veio Pou ~

*L*ong before gramophones became decorative pieces, I had my first impressionable encounter with the record player. I must have been just a curious six- or seven-year-old when our next-door neighbour brought one for Christmas. He was my friend's oldest brother, the first government employee from the family living in Imphal, the capital city of Manipur. It was fascinating to see how a box with a pin placed on a disc could generate such great music! Listening to the sound emanating from the cone-shaped tube reminded me of the lovely trumpet flower that grew in our front garden.

In all my memories, music has always been the best

way to usher in the Christmas season. All-time Christmas favourites by Boney M, ABBA, Jim Reeves and other popular singers would ring out from different corners of Khyoubu, the village where I was born. Literally translated as 'the moon place' in my native language, Poumai Naga, the name is derived from a legend, which says that there was once a glowing moon-shaped object in my village. In course of time, the precious item was taken away to another village, but it did not glow anymore. Perhaps, its rightful place was in Khyoubu. The legend also says that the last place where it glowed was Khyouchi, the peak of the highest hill in my village, thus earning it the name 'the house of the moon'.

Located on a small hilltop perched on a mountain range in the northern district of Manipur, Khyoubu appears to be a thin strip of land when one looks down from Khyouchi. To be up there is breathtaking because the aerial view allows the eye to scan many neighbouring villages as well. With two deep gorges on either side marking its natural boundary and the paddy fields surrounding it, my village spreads out like an exquisite tapestry that no artist could possibly paint. The southern end is a dense forest that houses a specific oak-like tree, whose fruit attracts a variety of migratory birds all through winter. The northern end opens to a layer of blue mountains, the span of which is endless. This is also the window for both the cool and the chilly winds to sweep through the length of Khyoubu.

Nights being extremely cold, basking in the morning

sun is something people look forward to every day. The silvery frost glittering in the distant foothills and the highland that meets the eyes of the early risers soon melts to reveal fresh green leaves, glowing as if they were bathed in cool waters. As the day progresses, one gets to see the clear blue sky and the wandering clouds—a marker of winter weather.

It is, however, the late afternoon sky that enchants me, especially during Christmas time. As the sun slowly makes its way to the western hills, one can see the gigantic trees playing with its rays. The long shadows spreading over the land makes a surreal picture of flattened trees and human beings alike. And as the sun sinks in slow motion, the rays are lifted to the sky, creating an orange tinge that spreads all across the horizon. This coincides with the greyish smoke curling upwards from the corners of houses, signalling the progress in the kitchens. The thatched roofs in the village make this scene even more homely. The grey smoke encountering the last rays of the sun in the sky builds up to a sensational moment for the beholder. It is like one of those last goodbyes that is difficult to utter, though deep inside you know the inevitability of meeting again the next day. Perhaps, it is the Christmas music echoing through my village at around the same hour that makes this time of the day even more sentimental.

Music has a way of lifting up one's spirits, and yes, of setting the mood for the festive season. The battery-run mike system with its two large horn speakers directed at both ends of Khyoubu would ring out with classic songs in the past. Today, the village has electricity, but in the days when the acid battery was the only source available to run the PA system, one would be judicious about its usage.

It was not unusual to hear Christmas songs blaring from cassette players by the end of October. The post-harvest life of the villagers is usually a restful period, mostly spent in a recreational mood until the next cycle of agricultural activities begins in the new year. With the winter setting in, this is also the time for families to garner themselves into spending time together, while shopping for warm clothes at the same time. For the monetarily weak population, buying new clothes for the upcoming festive season ends up being the only major time of the year to improve their wardrobes. This is one season when parents are willing to give in to their children's demands and choices. No wonder, as kids, we used to look forward to this time of the year eagerly!

For a communitarian village life, every festivity is a social event. But more than any other festival, Christmas is much grander in nature. Even those who stayed in town for various reasons would want to spend Christmas in the village. For students like me studying in the nearby towns, winter holidays were the ultimate treat. The year-long school calendar would come to a close, making one feel like a bird released from a cage. It was a joyous time. With no homework to worry about or uniforms to button up in the morning, every day would be a celebration. I remember my sense of excitement of going home for vacations being so high that even the three-and-a-half-hour walk on foot did not seem like a bother. But at the end of the long vacation (that seemed so short), it was always dreadful to think of the journey back to town for school on the same route. With no properly motorable road, walking long distances to catch a bus plying on a connecting highway was the only way to reach the nearest towns. Things are better now with passenger vehicles plying between towns and villages, which spare people the trouble of covering the long-winding roads across hillocks on foot.

One of the beautiful things that makes Christmas in the village special is that everyone works in unison for the success of the days-long celebrations. By early December, activities slowly build up. The social nature of the festivity perfectly suits the close-knit society where everyone's contribution is recognised. And this is made possible because there is delegation of responsibilities. Each family is required to contribute a few essential resources, some of which comes in the form of firewood required for community feasts and social gatherings, and other structural materials for the campsite. As always, the big campsite would be in the middle of Khyoubu, a public space convenient for such community gatherings. But it would wear a different look at Christmas because a temporary circular enclosure would be constructed with split bamboo to shield people from the harsh winter chill. This is where the community feast would be held before sundown.

Community feasts are organised in a participatory manner. First, a set of families would be identified as 'Christmas host families' of the year, which is a practice done on a rotational basis so that every family gets a turn only after a cycle of a few years. This way, the economic burden is lightened. Second, the preparation for each meal is undertaken by the different 'houses' formed specifically for the festive season. With a spirit of competitiveness instilled in everyone, the labour of hosting the entire population of a few hundreds is performed with joy. Rows of huge cauldrons cooking a variety of meats, chiefly pork and beef, over the makeshift fireplace would be a delight to watch. The aroma was irresistible! I have always enjoyed watching the intent activity of people engaged in preparing different items like chutneys, salads and steaming vegetables. Winter vegetables are considered tastier—perhaps, the frost at night blesses them with a distinctive flavour! Besides, the abundant edible plants and herbs from the forest would find their way to decorate the plates of the happy consumers at the feast. It is a pleasure to watch the excitement on the faces of the young and the old as they march into the campsite for dinner.

The feast is followed by an evening of getting together and socialising. This is a time of fun-filled activity—some choosing to showcase their talents through songs, some performing dramas and other forms of entertainment. The huge bonfires inside the campsite add a special warmth to the evening. For a village community, this time of fellowship shows the spirit of oneness and belonging, which is expressed through the language of love understood by all.

An important feature of Christmas is the spiritual aspect of it. After all, Christmas celebrations are rooted in the Bible. It is not just the nativity scene that is narrated through the plays enacted or the songs sung together, but the very nature of the message of Christmas delivered through the sermons in the church services. As a tradition, the church programmes are solemn and enriching spiritually—it feels like communing with the Divine. The Christmas story is essentially about God coming down to bring peace, harmony and joy to the world. And in that message is the model to heal all wrongs and conflicts—after all, we continue to live in an imperfect world with imperfect people. In that sense, the Christmas message is about hope—the hope of a future healed of disharmony and conflict. It is a wonder that every Christmas the message comes alive like a new story being told for the very first time. Perhaps, it is the forgetfulness of human beings that calls for a timely reminder. And Christmas comes along every year to do just that.

I have always marvelled at how Christmas time fits in perfectly with a village community life. The year-end time of reflection through the story of Jesus coming to earth to right wrongs provides people a chance for introspection on their personal relationships. For a largely Christian village like mine, it is these filial relations that shape the social outlook—everyone is somehow related to each other. Though far apart during most of the year,

Christmas time brings families together. It is this bond that families enjoy, a sense of belonging, that ultimately makes a home. I remember the first time I spent Christmas away from my family—it was no celebration at all. An emptiness gnawed at me. It was then that I realised that there is an innate mechanism that makes us want to be a part of one's family. However, that experience also made me understand the plight of orphans or people with broken families who were all around me. I realised I had been a callous human being, oblivious to the pain and the suffering that many are forced to undergo on a daily basis.

It is during this restive year-end period that the hard-working population is rejuvenated physically. I have seen how people in the villages in the area work all year. Their agricultural life cycle starts by tilling the fallow paddy fields in the first month of the new year, which is swiftly followed by seed sowing by early spring. By the time the rains arrive in the second quarter of the year, they prepare for paddy transplantation. Much of the rainy season is spent caring for the various crops, some of which are ready to be enjoyed by then. Seasonal fruits are bountiful and varied, many of which come as blessings from nature. This is the best time for kids to collect wild berries and fruits from the forest.

The end of the paddy transplantation is celebrated with much excitement—a sort of a half-way mark completion. This mid-year festival called Laonii is also a time of much jubilation, with plenty of cultural shows and community feasting. I reckon that villagers have their own way of boosting their spirits in all that they do!

The months before the paddy harvest are interlaced with many other agricultural activities. These are also the months of enjoying the fruits of one's labour, the seeds of which are sown months earlier. And this is also the time farmers pray for favourable weather to keep their crops safe from heavy rain. The months of receding rain see a transformation of the landscape too. The green terrace fields slowly transform into a yellowish landscape. And by the time the rice paddies are bent with golden sheaves, the farmers know it is time to get ready for the harvest. The gentle wind plays with the ripened sheaves, producing a jingling music as they dash against each other. The rows of heavy-laden stalks bowing under their own weight is a heart-warming sight for farmers. And the distant view of the terrace fields ripe for harvest at this time is a rare picture of beauty. In season's providence, thus, the dry autumn sky becomes a favourable omen for cultivation to begin.

Rice being the staple food, the garnering of the year's produce into the giant bamboo barns in a corner of one's house gives a great sense of satisfaction—ensuring food security for the family. It is no surprise, therefore, that the number of baskets poured into the barn determines the success of a family's harvest—whether they can last till the next harvest. Other food items can be acquired even from the wild, if the need arises, but rice cannot be cultivated without sowing. So, the year's harvest is a metaphor for the state of village life. A bountiful harvest sets the mood for a peaceful winter and even for the year ahead. Some years, when the harvest is not satisfactory, it dampens the spirit of the approaching winter.

Perhaps, this is why the farming community puts its heart and mind into rice cultivation all through the year. From weeding to providing adequate water to trimming unwanted plants or grasses on the terraces to protecting them from pests (birds and animals included), extreme care is taken to tend the paddy fields.

Regardless of the harvest results, there is a mechanism in place, which ensures a kind of equilibrium for all families. Every village installs a storehouse where each family contributes a portion according to their produce, in the discipline of Christian tithing (giving away one-tenth of one's earnings). This common pool is utilised in distributing a certain portion to the poor and the needy, selling this at a subsidised amount to those in need and reserving the rest for hosting guests of the church or for special occasions in the village. This principle manages to neutralise the effects of economic divide that could easily seep in.

In essence, the spirit of Christmas in the village is epitomised by the bonding that becomes visible at both the family and the community levels. This holds true for all the surrounding villages in the area. Though the decorations at home, the campsite and church are activities that excite everyone, they are mainly meant to boost the celebratory mood of coming together. The communitarian life gains a unique flavour at this time. And because the message of Christmas is about harmony, the song of the heavenly host singing 'peace on earth and goodwill to all' holds a special meaning.

Christmas tree installation in Nagaland.

Yuletides of Yore

Memories of High-altitude Christmases in Kodai, Valparai and Darjeeling

~ Minoo Avari ~

KODAIKANAL, 1990s

'Ponytail Gopi' and His Annual Party at the Kodai Club Badminton Court

As far as Christmases go in Kodaikanal, the only one of note was the party organised by Gopi. Ponytail Gopi as he was known, was a charismatic chap; a chef in his own right and someone with a flair for the elaborate. His party at the Badminton Court was quite an extraordinary effort. It was a sit-down affair. Dixie Prince and I were in charge of just one thing: Serviettes! Not knowing what to do, we went to Margaret Sekhran and she lent us a book.

Well, the serviettes had to be starched, to begin with. Then the book proceeded to illustrate how they were to be folded. These operations varied with the nature of the artist's intentions: from peeling a banana to making a swan. There were drawings, with complete instructions, of cut and sculpted pineapples and some floral stuff that resembled pansies.

It was great fun. My clumsy fingers were all over the place but Dixie sweetly helped out and we soon got a respectable table going, full of different serviette designs. Very fashionable indeed!

Dinner was served in stages; the food, drink and ambience par excellence. I forget what the dessert was but it would undoubtedly have been something exotic. That was far and away the best Christmas dinner I have had in Kodaikanal. There were one or two at the golf club but those were more spirited affairs and I doubt anybody remembers the food. Personally, I don't think there was any.

Otherwise, it was either lunch or dinner in people's houses and one extravaganza on my estate in Pethuparai. That ended quite wildly at Peggy Rustomji's place, where her son, Reshad, had insisted we end Christmas Day. There were no bison to contend with then and the few elephants that made occasional forays into the area prudently left us alone.

~

VALPARAI, 1973

Brandy, Pachyderms and a Pile of Dung: Santa at the Annamalai Club

It was the day of the annual Christmas party in Valparai. Dr Benjamin was slated to be Santa Claus. The president of the Annamalai Club, G.P. Reddy, was elated; Dr Benjamin, a well-rounded gentleman, would make the perfect Father Christmas. It was a beautiful evening and planters were playing tennis and golf under a sky that heralded the end of the monsoon.

At the last instant, however, Dr Benjamin called the president to say he couldn't take on the main role as he had a stomach ache. Playing Santa in front of forty or so kids of assorted ages is a daunting task. Who would volunteer to be Santa at the last minute? The beleaguered president rushed around in a frenzy. As further inducement, a bottle of brandy was offered. Still, there didn't seem to be any candidates.

Finally, he induced one of the golfers, in the last throes of a bad round, to quit the game. The brandy was sufficient temptation, and, with the help of two fellow golfers, the new Santa demolished the bottle. Santa, who was Aban Sethna's cousin, was dressed and ready—traditional red robes, white whiskers flowing down to the chest and coming to rest over a large pillow strapped under the garment—when he began to raise a request.

'I didn't get my full share of the brandy,' stated the worthy, saying that he was not going to be Santa under these circumstances. The flabbergasted president, who incidentally was the doppelganger of Omar Sharif, protested loudly—but as the would-be Santa had started disrobing, he immediately sent for another bottle of the much-desired amber fluid.

Fully sated, Santa left the changing room at last, making his way across the cricket pitch with his friends. A slanting sun silhouetted a very large object looming on the mud road to the Masonic Lodge. A horrified Santa found himself suddenly confronted by a huge elephant. Moreover, it had a chair strapped to its back!

By then a crowd from Valparai town had assembled around the elephant: kids gesticulated and squealed in delight, while a slender mahout tried to keep them at bay with a series of yells and threatening gestures.

Realising that Santa was never going to mount the pachyderm on his own steam, the villagers got together. Lifting the flummoxed Santa, they pushed him onto the chair atop the elephant. Nobody knows whose fault it was, but the chair had not been fastened properly and flipped over to the other side, taking Santa with it.

Lying sprawled on his belly, rocking on the pillow stuffed under his belt, Santa could not even utter a curse. The wind blown from his sails, he was hoisted, once again, atop the towering beast.

They had miscalculated yet again. Santa found himself astride the coarse hair that sticks out from an elephant's back. It was like riding a porcupine! Before he could protest, the elephant began its interminable journey (all of 500 yards) to the club house above.

But the surfeit of alcohol had finally kicked in. A weary and battered Santa put his elbows on the backrest of the chair, and fell asleep to the swaying gait of the elephant. At the destination, he awoke, but insisted he wouldn't get off the elephant at the entrance of the club. There was pandemonium as the elephant entered the club and, annoyed at the treatment being meted out, discharged a voluminous quantity of steaming dung.

The kids insisted this was the best Christmas ever and, after the presents were distributed, Santa was the life of the party!

A few years later, in the coffee belt of South Coorg, the same Santa, now acknowledged as Saint Nick himself, was called to perform above and beyond the call of duty. There was no elephant this time and the committee of Coorg ladies and gentlemen decided that Santa would make his appearance on roller skates. Well, I suppose everyone is entitled to surmise how that ended!

Postscript—The author was the Santa at the Annamallai Club. Aban is his father's sister's daughter.

~

DARJEELING, 1949

A Quiet Christmas

By the time the bells of St Andrews struck four times, it was dark. There weren't too many people in the town square, making it look even bigger than usual. It was bitterly cold too. Overcoats, scarves, gloves and felt hats made it difficult to recognise anyone: they looked huge in the pullovers and cardigans used as extra padding.

St Andrews overlooked Victoria Park, which is now a large building for political use. On the other side, it towers over the Gymkhana Club which, in turn, overlooks the Government House, used by the Governor of Bengal during the summer months. The Capitol Theatre and St Andrews Church, at opposite ends of the town, are iconic buildings, recognised by anyone who has visited Darjeeling.

I was very young at the time but the Planters, who were mostly British then, were the dominant socialites. The Planter's Club was the place to be for social recognition, and the Gymkhana Club for the Queen's birthday dance.

Of course, the Gymkhana Club did more than host the Queen's dinner and dance party. It had tennis courts and a skating rink the size of two tennis courts. The wooden flooring was Burma teak and made for a wonderful surface for roller skates to glide over. It was the destination for the hoi polloi. The skating rink housed a bandstand where waltzes, tangos and foxtrots were played and skaters would circle the floor in tune to the music. Those days Georgie Banks (Louis Banks' father) would switch between the clarinet and the trumpet even as old man Coutinho sawed away at the violin. The drums were the domain of Mr Wilson.

I still remember Edgar Cleaver playing the accordion through the early and mid 1950s. My mother never spent Christmas in Kodai. It was too quiet for her! She was the life and soul of parties at home in Darjeeling and later at the Coonoor Club, playing the piano, singing, and dancing…She was an excellent dancer.

Tonight, there was no discernible breeze. Yet the cold, coming off the mountain range, chilled one to the marrow. Some folks were busy scratching their noses, fingers and other assorted extremities in an attempt to ward off the bane of winter; literally doing St Vitus' dance to get temporary relief from itchy chilblains.

Every alternate year, the skies chose to remain overcast. It wasn't as bitterly cold then, under an overcast sky, but as it turned completely dark, snow started falling. It was never very heavy. Tiny flakes floated down, each with its own distinctive design, until a sudden flurry turned everything pristine white.

Crunching through the white carpet, holding my mother's hand, I was excited. Muriel Ray had invited us for Christmas dinner and my mother was on a last-minute mission to buy presents. Some shops were open and Habib Mallik, on Chowrasta Square, was the destination.

It was warm inside. Fur coats and an assortment of warm garments, hanging from the ceiling, left a musty smell within the confines. Trinkets from Tibet were displayed on large tables and collapsible walnut tables, carved intricately, from Kashmir took pride of place. There were thick Tibetan carpets with a multitude of designs covering the walls, and there was even a hookah in a far corner. I think it was for sale.

With an experienced eye, my mother took in all the

wares on offer. I wasn't aware of what she finally settled on because a large foldable knife had caught my attention. With all the curiosity of a four-year-old, I stared at this wonderful invention, wondering what marvellous things I could do with it. Before I could ask her to buy it for me, she had finished her purchases and dragged me out of the shop.

The disappointment was soon forgotten. Snow was still falling and, in the silence, faint Christmas carols came from a ragtag bunch of school children. A girl in front carried a hurricane lantern and six or seven behind joined her to sing 'Ave Maria' softly into the night. There was nothing rag-tag about their singing; it sounded as though the angels were amongst us.

We passed other groups on our way home. In the dark, trampling over a carpet of snow, the enchantment of hearing 'Silent Night' was certainly the nearest thing to heaven I had ever experienced...And then my mother opened her lips, her beautiful voice floating over the whitened earth, and I thought I was in heaven.

At the entrance to our doorway another group awaited our arrival. As soon as they saw us they burst out with 'Happy Birthday'. I clutched my mother's hand tighter. She was twenty-eight years old that Christmas day. To me, she was very old and I was afraid I wouldn't have her with me much longer. Intuitively, my mother turned to me and told me to hurry and get ready for the evening party.

The nightmare of mortality wiped away, we arrived at the huge hacienda that housed Muriel and her daughter

Jennifer. The extensive lawn had turned white, and the tiny pond in the centre, frozen solid. In the years to follow that Christmas of 1949, I was to become familiar with the hacienda. After the Rays left, it housed the Plant family from Burma, before being converted into a communist commune!

The sitting room was large and there was a roaring fire, which did more to light up the room than the dim electric bulbs overhead. There was an entire goose, still steaming, on the table and a white swan hanging from the rafters. It was enough to give me goosebumps. Turning to my father, I pointed to it and he said it was a 'khoya bag', which didn't make any sense to me at the time.

After the goose was carved, the stuffing attacked and all the crackling chewed, aunt Muriel pulled a cord from under the overhead swan. As the belly ripped, confetti drizzled all over the dining table. There was an occasional thud and my parents reached out to discover what surprises they held. I got into the act and quickly discovered a tiny car. It was a model of a Hillman Minx.

It had two doors which opened. Inside there were seats, a steering wheel and a dashboard. Dad looked at it and told me it was an expensive Dinky Toy. I treasured it for many years. I was drowsy by then and fell asleep. I don't remember how I got home but was told later that dad had carried me back.

My dreams of delicious marzipan, English toffees and Dundee bread were interrupted when I remembered Jenny kissing me and wishing me a Merry Christmas. I awoke rubbing my cheek. After all, which four-year-old wants to be kissed, Christmas or no Christmas.

She had also added, 'This is specially for your mother's birthday.' My mother was a Christmas baby and this was the first of many, many Christmas memories I have. It was a very special one indeed.

Afterword: On the first of October 2021 my mother passed away. She would have been one hundred years that Christmas.

A Village Christmas

~ Damodar Mauzo ~

Translated from the Konkani by Jerry Pinto

There are two Goan festivals that I truly enjoy. The first is Chawath (or Ganesh pooja) and the second is Christmas. I love the Ganesh festival because many people from the neighbourhood visit our home, and I love Christmas because we visit many people's homes during the Christmas week. All festivals are occasions to spread joy and so are these two. Happiness has the rare ability to grow when it is shared.

There are some other things that both these festivals have in common. What comes to my mind first are neoris (deep-fried sweet pastries, like the gujiyas of northern India) and crackers, both of which were delights when

I was a boy. I remember as Chawath approached our family would send neoris to our Christian friends in the neighbourhood and when Christmas came around, our Christian neighbours would send us neoris and cake. Personally, I was not very fond of neoris but I loved the batatyachi kaapaa (a potato sweet) that came with the festival of Ganesha and the doce (gram sweet) that came with the festival of Christ's birth. As a child, I knew that at Christmas other delicious offerings would come my way: dodol (a pudding of rice, jaggery and coconut), baath (a coconut cake), ghos (tender coconut crusted with sugar), bebinca and of course Christmas cake. This was no less than a feast. No wonder that as a child, I longed for these festivals to come. That hasn't changed.

When I grew up, I was a shopkeeper by profession. Christmas therefore had a special significance for me. My father had set up our shop, the first shop to come up in the village and for long the biggest in the Majorda area. He died when I was twelve years old and for some years my uncle ran the shop for us. Then I took over and ran it for forty-six years. The shop was always at its busiest in the Christmas season. The people of my village—and of the panchkroshi, the five neighbouring villages—expected to find everything they needed under one roof. And they did; we had a greater range to offer in our shop than you will find in any contemporary 'superstore'. Apart from regular groceries, we stocked umbrellas, needle-and-thread, cotton wicks, oil fresh from the press, baalshep (a variety of badishep to relieve stomach gas in children), sanitary napkins, nappies and scores of other items of regular use. If someone had died in the family, the bereaved would come to us for white gloves, white lace and kerchiefs. In some cases the burial had to be delayed so that relatives living far away might be able to attend the funeral. Then denatured spirit would be injected into the veins of the body to slow down the processes of decomposition. Needless to say, we stocked denatured alcohol as well. And if despite these precautions the body began to decompose, we had eucalyptus oil and perfume spray to smother the odours of decay.

I remember being roused from slumber one late night by a knocking on the door. When I opened it, there stood Dr Luis Prot Barbosa, who was later to become the chief minister of Goa. At the time, he was a practicing physician and had come from the village Cansaulim, five kilometres away, where a death had occurred. I opened the shop and found him a bottle of denatured spirit. If the death had occurred in a Hindu household, they would need other things, like agarbattis, camphor, and even shrouds of white cotton. When there was an annual shraadh ceremony marking the departure of a family member, we knew that someone from the family would come for black cinnamon. When the auspicious full moon bloomed in the sky, people would change their janeus (sacred thread) and so we would stock those too. Catholic households would have the ladainhas—the litanies—and they would come to buy the betinas, the square pieces of black cloth that they would drape around their necks.

At Ekadashi, the eleventh day of the month, the demand for food that could be eaten on a fast day would rise. A wise shopkeeper would make sure he had enough moong daal laid in. Around Christmas, those who couldn't make baath and ghos for whatever reason, knew that these traditional sweets would be available at our shop.

At Christmas, it was also traditional for every family to set off some fireworks. These were of the quieter variety, unlike the 'rockets' and 'atom bombs' that were popular during the Chawath, the Ganesha festival. I remember that many Hindu residents of our village would go to their ancestral homes for Chawath, back to their villages in Ponda or Pernem or Cancona. But we still sold a great deal of fireworks—Christian men and women of the village would come with their children who would ask for 'atom bombs' and 'rockets' and 'flower pots'. Like Christmas, Chawath was everybody's festival.

So, when people call Majorda a Christian village, it angers me. Does a village have a religion? Can a village have a religion? When the village church turned four hundred years young, Father Nicholas Pereira, an intellectual and scholar who was the Principal of St Xavier's College, took it upon himself to write a history of our village. He told me that in the course of his research, he had happened upon a list of the gaonkars of the village at the time the church was being built; the name Somu Mauzo figured on that list. This told me that my family had been in the village for at least four hundred years, and prospered.

With the years, as the number of my friends in the village grew, the number of courtesy calls I had to pay at Christmas time also grew. If I failed in this, they took offence. But how could I visit their homes when the shop also had to be kept open? I could not very well turn my back on my customers, whose number went up greatly in the week starting 17th December. Finally, I thought up a solution. Thursday was my weekly closing day and I was very particular about this because I wanted to give time to my family. But in the week of Christmas, I kept the shop open on Thursday too, and that became the tradition. That one week the shop would remain open every single day. I would close it only on Christmas Eve. That way, my customers were happy, workers in the shop were happy, and my friends were happy too—because I was free to visit them for Christmas.

There are two friends whose homes I visit without fail on Christmas: Xavier Cota and Willy, a friend from Margao. After all these years, they are family to us. Willy's son Augustine shares a birthday with my daughter Meghna and they are like siblings. Xavier's nephew Sidney also thinks of Meghna as his sister and this is how he introduces her to people. When he was young, Sidney once introduced me to a visitor as 'My sister's father.' The visitor took some time to digest this. When Meghna was six or seven years old and studying in a school in Margao, her teacher asked her, 'How many uncles do you have?' Quick as a flash, Meghna answered: 'I have two uncles.' The teacher was surprised at this and wondered if Meghna had understood the question, for she knew that I had no brothers. Meghna explained: 'Xavier Uncle and Willy Uncle.'

When my eldest daughter Rupali came of age, she expressed the desire to go to midnight mass. She went with one of her closest friends, Lucy, and still remembers it as a precious experience. This was not done consciously; it was how things were in our village. When we went to America some years ago, we visited our friends from the village, Sidney and his brother Savio who had settled there. We stayed at Sidney's house. He remembered how he and Savio would come to celebrate Chawath with us. They would spend the day with us. They joined us when the afternoon aarti was performed. They cupped their hands and drank panchamrut and later sat on mats for the festive meal, eating off banana leaves as to the manor born...Our stay with Sidney in a distant land was a time of nostalgic remembering. When our children mingled, no one cared who was Christian or Hindu or Muslim. These markers of identity may have informed some community-specific social functions, but as families living close to each other, and during festivals and larger cultural events, all differences would melt away. We were all one. Of course, such attempts must be made from all sides. It did not matter who took the first step, and for most of us it still doesn't. And for this reason, among many others, I am proud of my village.

The people of the village are my people, because they have taken me as one of theirs too. I have lost count of the times I have been invited as the chief guest of house-warming ceremonies or even to raise the toast at Christian weddings. The vicar of our local church has often come to our home to eat poha and on occasions has also brought his friends with him. Around fifteen years ago, the late Dr U.R. Ananthamurthy, renowned author, came to visit us with his wife Esther. I took him to see our village church, which we call Mhamai Saaibini. When the vicar saw us, he came outside to greet us. When I introduced Dr Ananthamurthy, he showed him around the church himself. Dr Ananthamurthy was very impressed by this. When we met later in Delhi he made it a point to talk about the beauty of the confessionals in the church, the filigree work of the wood, and the affection and respect shown me by a Catholic priest.

It is this feeling that is priceless; it is our true inheritance and treasure. When some people try to divide us on the basis of our religions, this intolerance damages the whole fabric of our society. This othering hurts the health of our community. We have to live as one. We must learn to hold together, to respect the traditions of unity and amity which will hold intolerance and religious hatred at bay. And what better time to demonstrate this than at Ganesh pooja, Diwali, Eid and Christmas? These are all times of happiness and we must share our happiness and spread it. It is what our village has done for centuries.

How India's Pluralistic Past Shows the Way Forward

~ Manimugdha S. Sharma ~

On 1st December 1581, a rather gruesome spectacle played out in the manor of Tyburn in Middlesex County, England. Three Catholic Jesuit priests, the most noteworthy among them being the future Saint Edmund Campion, were dragged out, then 'hanged, drawn and quartered'—a phrase that implied hanging and brutalisation of the body. If you have watched Mel Gibson's *Braveheart* and how his character, William Wallace, is executed, you will have some idea how that went.

They were the latest (but not the last) victims of Queen Elizabeth Tudor's zealous persecution of Catholics in her realm. At the same time, half a world away in Fatehpur Sikri, the court of Emperor Jalaluddin Muhammad Akbar was engaging with Portuguese Jesuit priests to understand and appreciate their faith even as the imperial ateliers were busy painting Nativity scenes on canvas. What resulted from this was an amazing cultural efflorescence that fused the traditions of the two most dominant world religions—Christianity and Islam—and, as one historian put it, 'the most visually potent figural iconography ever devised by a Muslim power'.

Christianity had been in India for much longer. There are two very different apocryphal traditions about the coming of Christianity to India.

The first one (also the less familiar one) says Thomas the Apostle arrived in the court of Indo-Parthian king Gondophernes (believed to have ruled from 19-45 CE) and introduced the new faith in north-western and northern India. The other tradition says Thomas came to what is today Kerala in 52 AD and built the first church there and introduced the faith. Christians today believe in the second tradition more. Historians often doubt these stories about Doubting Thomas, but the historical record seems to suggest the presence of Christian settlements in India by the fourth century CE.

The Christian tradition also tells us that Saint Thomas was martyred about twenty years after he first arrived in India, at a place in modern-day Chennai that is now called St Thomas Mount, and his mortal remains were entombed at Santhome (Mylapore) where a grand church, the San Thome Basilica, stands today. The Portuguese built it in the sixteenth century, replacing another older church that had somehow become a revered place for not just Christians but also Muslims and Hindus. The Venetian traveller Marco Polo had, in the thirteenth century, written that the Muslims revered St Thomas as one of their own and a great prophet. About thirty years later, Italian Franciscan friar Odoric of Pordenone, visiting St Thomas Mount, found the church filled with Hindu idols. Then, in the sixteenth century, before the Portuguese took over the place and built their church, one of their pastors, Duarte Barbosa, found the church deserted except for a Muslim fakir who was managing the place and lighting a lamp there every day.

It is not known if Barbosa appreciated the fact that a Muslim fakir was taking care of a Christian shrine. But less than a century later, another Portuguese would record for posterity how Christian celebrations were flourishing in the court of the Muslim Timurid emperor, who was called Shahanshah-i Hindustan, and whom some Hindus had started describing as an avatar of Vishnu.

Jesuit priest Jerome Xavier was in Lahore, the new capital of the Mughal Empire, in 1597 when he documented how Christmas was celebrated by the Mughals: a description that someone sitting in Lahore, or Delhi, or Guwahati today will be able to relate to in some ways. 'At Christmas (1597) our brother Benedict de Goes prepared a manger and cradle as exquisite as those of Goa itself, which heathens (read Hindus) and

Muhammadans, as well as Christians, thronged to see. In the evening masses were said with great ceremony, and a pastoral dialogue on the subject of the Nativity was enacted by some youths in the Persian tongue, with some Hindustani proverbs interspersed (*adjunctis aliquot Industani sententiis*),' Xavier wrote.

He continued, 'At the conclusion of the sacred office, the gates were opened to all: and such was the piety of the throng of Heathen and Muhammadans that on seeing the child Jesus lying in the cradle they bowed themselves to the ground in worship. Such was the crowd of spectators in those days that the cradle was kept open till the eighth day after Epiphany—the fame of the spectacle spread through the town and brought even outsiders to see the sight.'

The following year, the crib was kept open to the public for twenty days as three or four thousand people daily came to view it. By 1600, the three Magi and 'figures of certain Prophets' were added to the Nativity scene 'with copies in Persian of their prophecies of the birth of Christ'. Experts were brought from Goa who used 'hydraulic inventions' to add glitter to the scene: 'artificial birds which sang, images of apes which spouted water from their eyes and mouths, figures of Magi which wept tears and so forth,' writes Sir Edward Maclagan in his 1932 work, *The Jesuits and the Great Mogul*.

Pierre du Jarric, another Jesuit, tells us about the display of a painting of 'Our Lady', copied from an original in Rome, at the church in Lahore during Christmastide in 1601-1602 and people from all walks of life thronging the church to see the painting. Jarric claims daily attendance exceeded 10,000 people! Emperor Akbar had the painting brought to his palace where he treated it with great reverence and showed it to his harem. He arranged a special viewing for his mother, Hamida Bano Begum.

It also appears from Xavier's writings that the Christian festivals were only becoming more popular with each passing year. He wrote again in 1604, 'The feasts of Christmas and Easter are kept at Lahore with great solemnity, and the church being so large and beautiful, everything can be well carried out. Joao Battista (a Florentine man)…was present at one of these feasts and wept with joy to see these things done openly in a land of Muhammadans.'

In 1610, Xavier observed in Agra that the crib was kept open for public viewing for forty days, and one day, he counted the visiting crowd to be 14,000 strong. Maclagan comments that this was quite something as 'no jubilee or feast in Europe, we are told, was ever so frequented.' Xavier also observed that more Hindus were coming with offerings, and at least one woman he had spoken with had said that she was blessed with a son as she had asked 'Bibi Mariam' (Mother Mary) to bless her with one, and she had come to give thanks. This cross-faith appeal of Christian holy figures has only grown over the centuries, as has the popularity of Christmas in India.

In his last post on Facebook in April 2021, my father, Surendra Kumar Sharma, shared a photo of Christ and asked the Lord to save us all from the pandemic. My wife and I had tested positive for Covid-19, and my father was very worried about us. Days later, he was in the hospital and went down fighting the virus. But the fact that a Hindu man turned to the Christian 'Son of God' to save his family says something about the syncretic tradition of this country.

Today, the popularity of Christmas has grown so much that it has almost attained a secular character. It is common for non-Christians to sign off with a 'Merry Christmas' greeting or to instal a Christmas tree and a star at their homes. Even when these are missing, eating a special dinner on the day, or hanging decorative lights from balconies is common.

A lot of it has to do with pop culture and mass media. After all, Hollywood taught us to say 'Jesus Christ!' in unpleasant or difficult situations; or long for a serendipitous meeting with that special someone on Christmas like in the noughties hit, *Serendipity*; or nurse heartbreak by listening to George Michael's 'Last Christmas'. For so many of us, this has been part of our growing-up experience.

Unfortunately, this syncretism built over centuries, is now under attack from a virulent politics of hate, which sees pluralism as an albatross around the republic's neck. No wonder then that attacks on churches and church-run institutions are on the rise, and vigilante groups now openly threaten believers and non-believers alike for celebrating 'foreign festivals' like Christmas.

Perhaps Christmas should also become an occasion when the nation needs to pledge to reclaim its pluralism.

Christmas Pakwan

~ Jaya Bhattacharji Rose ~

Every Christmas, my paternal grandmother, Dadi, would begin preparing the pakwan. It was a process that took a few weeks of preparation, followed by a few days of intense cooking. The original owners of Dadi's house were British. It had a kitchen with an inbuilt wood oven but it was outside the house, as in most British houses of the time, so that the cooking could be done outside. The house still exists. Dadi later built a kitchen and a pantry attached to the dining room. She had a fairly large family. All of us would look forward to the Christmas lunch when the dining table was groaning with food—cold meats, shami kababs, chicken curry, pulao with kaju and caramelised onions on top, raita, gajar ka halwa, zarda, fruits. Dadi was a hospitable lady, so she would also take into account the endless stream of guests who had to be fed.

Our house was in the Cantonment area in Meerut, where Dadi had built two prominent schools. So, we had Army personnel, students (past and present), parents, teachers, and many more from the town who would come to greet her and the family on Christmas Day. The visitors came from all walks of life. If they came during the day, they were received in the front lawn. Dadi was an incredible gardener too, so the garden would be ablaze with winter blooms! The guests were served various homecooked delicacies. There was always something for everyone, irrespective of their dietary restrictions, especially if they belonged to another faith. No one left our place unfed. If they came in the evening, they would be received in the drawing room, inevitably around the fireplace which was constantly being stoked by a pile of wooden logs placed next to Dada and Dadi's chairs. A tray with bowls of sinfully delicious eats was placed conveniently in front of the visitors.

Dadi's kitchen was buzzing with activity throughout the year. There were maids constantly scurrying about, cutting and chopping, cooking and serving. In the midst of this hustle-bustle, sat Dadi on her wooden chair. She was too large and overweight to move around with ease! She would supervise the proceedings and kept a sharp eye on all the food being cooked. She was very particular about how the dishes were prepared. The larder keys were with her and if any ingredient was required, the cupboard would be opened in her presence and the precise amount of masala or oil doled out. Other provisions, including the onions, potatoes and sugar, were stored in her bedroom or under her bed! No wonder we had situations where a particularly flighty maid chopped up Dadi's precious gladioli bulbs assuming they were large onions.

Come December, there was a different buzz in the air. Dadi would organise the staff in such a manner that all the stoves were in operation—gas cylinder and the mud angeethis that required handmade coal balls. The pantry would be cleaned thoroughly, sheets laid out on the floor and maids seated, working intently on their assigned chores. There was humming and chattering but the dishes were cooked with precision. At times, it was like an assembly line. If samosas were to be made, then one maid would be rolling the dough, another cutting and filling, and the third frying both kinds of samosas—keema and meetha. The samosas would then be cooled and placed in the wooden and wire mesh doli and locked. Dadi herself would be sitting on a chair with her coal-fuelled mud angeethi beside her. She did not like cooking on the gas stove. On the angeethi would be placed the large dekchis, one by one, and she would cook khope ka keema, gajar ka halwa, zarda and other dishes.

The festive season would be kickstarted by preparations for the dishes that required a longer lead time, like the Christmas cake and the cold meats. The meats were prepared by rubbing the legs of lamb with rock salt and grapefruit and placing them in earthen pots which would then be covered. Later, the meats would be boiled to remove the excess salt and slices of it would be served cold. For the Christmas cake, Dadi would take the assistance of Robert, a worker in my Dada's karkhana in Meerut, who would advise her on the quantities of fruit, candied peel, nuts, eggs and butter. Once the chopping was over, she would cut strips of brown paper to line the baking dishes. Tiny labels on which she had scribbled her initials—SB (Shakuntala Bhattacharji)—would be placed in the batter. Then the local baker would be summoned. He would arrive with a large parat (a large flat brass dish used for kneading dough, but useful for mixing large quantities of cake batter too). Into this, the fruits would be upturned, and the many eggs broken—after, of course, making sure that the brindled bull terrier Lobo was not stealing the eggs and squirrelling them away in his food bowl. He would carefully lift the nail from the doli's latch and remove the eggs one by one. He used to sit in the folds of Dadi's saree and as soon as he saw a chance, he would attack the doli. Bull terriers have powerful jaws that can kill—once they latch onto an animal, their jaws cannot be opened until the other animal is destroyed. And yet Lobo never broke an egg!

My Dadi had got the Christmas cake recipe from Robert. His father, Barkat, used to work as a cook in Lucknow for my maternal great-grandmother, Constance Dass, Principal of Isabella Thoburn College (1939-45). My maternal grandmother, Premilla Mukarji, Constance's daughter, used to speak of this cake recipe. Nani was a very good cook too, but it was always a laborious process with her. Whereas with Dadi, a warm, generous food hug was what she revelled in, even though it was not the mainstay of her existence. Teaching was. Dadi established schools that still exist. Robert gave my Dadi the recipe, much before my mother, Shobhana Bhattacharji, married into the family. Meanwhile, the recipe had travelled.

I inherited the same recipe from both sides of my family, but like all good recipes, it was open to many interpretations and variations. Dadi had adapted it to suit the morally correct palates and done away with the rum, increased the petha and reduced some of the rich masala. I do not recall Dadi adding spices. Her cake tasted like an ordinary fruit cake that existed in vast quantities but lacked the razzle-dazzle. When I read the recipe written by Constance Dass, the weights and measures were in seers and chhataks. Also, it was richer than I had imagined. The first couple of times I made the recipe I followed her instructions to the letter and the cake rose beautifully, especially when the egg whites were folded into the batter. No baking powder is required. The stiff egg whites do the needful. Slowly, I tweaked the recipe to soak the masala in rum. I prefer to do this in September and bake in December. In fact, I pickle vast quantities of the masala in a glass jar belonging to my great-grandmother, Badi Dadi or Mary Chandulal Mukarji, my mother's dadi. This is used in the cakes, mince pies and panettone too.

Badi Dadi was so called because my twin brother and I had to differentiate between the two dadis in our life. Badi Dadi was a tremendous cook herself, she had a fantastic kitchen in Dalhousie, using wood fire and box ovens to churn out magnificent meals with clockwork precision. There was no fussiness in her cooking.

I love the manner in which food histories get passed on from generation to generation through their use and through the stories that are told. Shakuntala Bhattacharji only transmitted recipes orally or she demonstrated a dish. Whereas Constance Dass and Mary Chandulal Mukarji wrote recipes—their recipe notebooks are a fine repository of food influences and regional cooking. I still consult them. The recipes also bring out the fact that an Indian Christian family did not observe any food taboos, so we had quite a selection of dishes. All tried and tested too! My mum, masi and I continue the tradition of writing recipes and have amassed quite a collection. It is still my go-to repository rather than the internet.

This Christmas cake recipe is the basis of a good wedding cake too. I made a 25 kg, five-tier cake, with homemade marzipan, royal icing and orange marmalade for my brother's wedding. I made everything from scratch, including the blessed marzipan by crushing almonds and kneading the dough till it rolled smoothly. My mother provided some of her to-die-for bittersweet marmalade with its fine slivers of translucent orange peel. Layering the cake with marmalade, marzipan and royal icing, I decorated it with tiny flowers made with icing sugar as well as lots of fresh flowers. It was so heavy that a special wooden cake stand had to be made. This cake preserves well for at least six months.

For my own wedding, I did not have the time to make the cake. My fiancé Jacob Rose brought sample pieces of cake to test. I was horrified. They tasted ghastly, nothing but ordinary cake being passed off as wedding cake! I insisted on meeting the baker, Philip. He came. A family consultation was held. Philip explained the process. I did not approve. So, I gave him my Christmas cake recipe and said, use this. He did and we had a delicious wedding cake. Philip used the recipe to turn around his Christmas cakes and became a huge commercial success. So much so that even *we* get slices of it at our church fellowship after midnight service. Philip modified the recipe further, to make it a commercially viable option. After his death, his nephew inherited the business, and the tradition continues. The recipe lives.

Today, I am probably one of the few, if not the only one, in my generation and in the extended clan who makes Christmas pakwan. The process begins weeks ahead. With time, I have modified the offerings to incorporate Jacob's tastes and childhood memories and create new ones for our daughter, Sarah Rose. So now I prepare Christmas cake, mince pies, panettone, pinnis with pumpkin seeds, panjiri, gujiyas, ginger cookies, shami kababs, khope ka keema, yakhni pullao, mathri with zeera, cinnamon rolls and more. Everything is homemade, including the desi ghee/clarified butter that I use in the panjiri and gujiyas. It is a juggling feat that calls for my professional publishing commitments, teaching, and cooking to dovetail into each other. How I manage is nothing short of a Christmas miracle!

We are Christians and have been for generations. It means we have recipes from across the country and relatives are to be found everywhere. The pakwan that we serve at home is an amalgamation of these experiences and is a fine testament to the syncretic nature of India. The recipes that we use can be found in Muslim, Hindu and Christian households. Ultimately, it does not matter which faith these foods originate from. What matters is the joy of cooking, providing hospitality, and watching others revel in the food hug!

The Christmas cake recipe below is what I have inherited, and adapted from seer and chhatak to kilos and grams. Also, it is really difficult to give measures as a lot of this is done by andaaz (instinct). Some like more ginger, others prefer more sultanas, etc. Some like to put petha, which I absolutely detest in cakes, and others prefer to use nuts and definitely not sliver the almonds. It really depends on what the cook desires.

Christmas Cake

INGREDIENTS

- ½ kg mixed peel cut fine (a little more peel can be put, if desired)
- 125 g preserved ginger
- ½ kg almonds, blanched and shelled, or use walnuts
- ½ kg raisins
- ½ kg sultanas

- 250 g currants (if you can get good ones, otherwise do not use)
- ½ kg fine flour
- ½ kg sugar (burn about 100 gms to get the dark colour of the cake)
- 20 eggs, good size, separated
- 1 kg butter
- 1 or 2 level tbsps ground spices (jaiphal, javetri, barri elaichi, dalchini, laung—all ground dry)

METHOD

1. Mix the sugar and butter together and beat until creamy.
2. Gradually add egg yolks, continue beating.
3. Once well beaten, add the flour a little at a time, beating all the time.
4. Add the mixed peel, preserved ginger, almonds, raisins, sultanas and currants.
5. Mix thoroughly.
6. Add a generous dash of brandy/sherry/rum now, if desired, or dribble later over baked cakes.
7. Lastly, fold in the stiffly beaten egg whites.
8. Put into baking dishes immediately.
9. Bake in a slow oven until the colour is a rich brown.

The Spirit of Christmas Cake
~ Priti David ~

'I hope you'll mention how everyone would swipe the dry fruits while chopping and try to polish off the rum meant to soak the raisins,' my cousin observed when I told him what I was writing. 'We always had to buy twice the required quantity,' he added, chuckling. In our family, Christmas cake brought joy long before it was unwrapped at Christmas time to become the symbol of good tidings and cheer to all men.

This grand annual production called for planning months ahead and everybody was expected to pitch in and do their bit for family honour. As young as eight years old, I remember sitting on upturned dalda tins in the dingy bakery and feeling mighty important as I wrote out our family name on strips of paper to be carefully placed atop the wobbling batter so that our cakes would not get mixed up in the oven.

The retired school teachers and military types enjoyed the bandobast (organising) while the matriarchs with superlative culinary skills saw this as the ultimate showpiece. Like in the making of jams and pickles, Christmas cake-making also saw random family members turn into connoisseurs and critics but only those with some stature in the family could expect to be heard.

At the beginning of November, post sermon, families would lean across the pews in church and whisper the question: 'How many kilos of cake this Christmas?' Those expecting large contingents of guests would hazard five kilos, which wait a moment, meant five kilos *each* of flour, fruit, unsalted butter and ghee and then at least two-and-a-half to three kilos of dry fruits and nuts—resulting in a gargantuan number of cakes for family and friends. My cousin says the Mukherjee-David record one Christmas was a 10 kg outlay, perhaps keeping in mind my parents' wedding a month later when a sample of the family Christmas cake was expected to create the right impression with the bride's family.

In keeping with the spirit of the season, the recipe for a Christmas cake is most forgiving. The Indian version is actually a close cousin of British plum pudding also served at Christmas time. Unlike their traditional plum pudding, our cake is not steamed and neither does it have lard. Instead, it is baked for a longish time in an oven and a combination of butter and ghee is used as shortening. Indian Christians add a generous dose of hot spices such as nutmeg, cinnamon, cloves and shahi zeera (royal cumin seeds); roasted dry and then ground and added, also referred to as 'cake masala'.

In Allahabad of the 1970s, when I was growing up, perishables like butter and eggs could not be bought off the shelf at one shot; fridges were a rarity as was the uninterrupted electricity to run it. If winter had set in you could manage to store a few days' worth of butter. The rest of the shortening would be made up by ghee which was readily available. A proper Christmas cake called for two dozen eggs per kilogram of flour, a mindboggling ratio necessary because of the weight of fruits. The small desi (country) eggs would be stored in earthen jars filled with lime water for up to a month. Every week, word would go to the nearby village that Doc Sahib's house needed eggs, and their weekly output would be thus commandeered.

'Cake shopping' heralded the start of the show and was always done in Chowk, the market hub of Allahabad. My parents, both busy doctors, would take an afternoon off to do the shopping, my father weaving the jeep through the narrow congested by-lanes, and my older brother and I vainly trying to keep the empty tins for ghee and fruit from rolling around and clattering at the back.

Both the quality and quantity of dry fruit and nuts was critical to the final outcome. The accepted ratio of flour to nuts was 1:3. Raisins formed the mainstay and both the tiny currants and the larger sultanas were first to be ticked off the list. Peels were important for their colour and fruity flavour and my mother had to look the other way at the artificial colouring. After the dry fruit was washed and aired, it was time for the chopping and dicing. The most honest volunteers, the ones least likely to nibble their way through were given the expensive walnuts, pine nuts and almonds to handle.

Chopping of peels on the other hand, was a downright lowly task. The strips of orange peel in unnatural shades of bright green and orange were sticky from the sugar syrup they were soaked in. Dicing them was not as easy as you may think as they tended to slither all over the cutting board evading your knife and leaving a trail of sticky juice on your fingers. So, the young ones who wanted to help were usually given this task till they tired and ran off.

A special ingredient in the cakes in north India was the translucent petha—cubes of white pumpkin soaked in sugar syrup and resembling Turkish delight in both flavour and texture. Petha, chopped into tiny cubes, added just the right shot of cloying sweetness and the tiny cubes of translucent whiteness held their own in the brown batter.

On D-day—baking day, preparations would begin by mid-morning, and lunch would be quickly dispatched with. Lists were gone over thoroughly; nothing could be allowed to go wrong. Sugar those days was quite coarse and had to be ground before mixing into the batter. The spice masala was readied and the rest of the ingredients now emerged from the storeroom. Most large families had their own baking tins and these were cleaned and lined with butter-paper trimmed to size. Till the 1960s, the baker would come home to do the mixing and then cart the ready batter away, but later it was all done at the bakery itself.

The best slot was early December as this allowed the cake to sit for two-three weeks before Christmas Day for the flavours to intensify. The preferred time was 5 p.m. when the oven had cooled down a bit after the intense heat needed for the regular bread and buns. The subsequent low, steady heat of the wood-fired ovens allowed the fruit to cook and promised a gentle crust with an evenly baked crumb.

Camp was set up in the baking room, the warm light from the oven bouncing on the dark tins and casting a magical spell on an early winter evening. The baker would be seated on the ground, surrounded by our store of eggs, butter, ghee, flour, sugar and dry fruits within easy reach. The family members stood or perched on whatever they could find. The mixing would begin, the baker expertly breaking up the butter and ghee using his hand as a whip to combine the ground sugar. One hand was strictly for mixing and with the other he would break the eggs in one by one, both hands never touching each other and working in a rhythmic motion.

'Gosh, we forgot the caramel!' and then there would be a mad scramble. Most bakers had a small kerosene stove which could be fired up to make the caramel—a delicate affair, which lent the cake its lovely golden hue. Too dark was frowned upon as it could get bitter and spoil the flavour. After the butter, ghee, sugar and eggs had been well whipped, the flour and cake masala would be sieved in followed by the cooled caramel and the dry fruits, rum and all. Some of the batter would be kept aside before adding the fruit—these made up the 'second' cakes without fruit ostensibly for those who were not fond of it, but also for the less deserving! Altogether an expensive production, nothing was to be wasted, so to the scraps of dough sticking to the mixing bowl were added a few eggs and jaggery to fashion Christmassy-flavoured festive biscuits.

My great-grandfather the venerable Dr B.K. Mukherjee's Christmas offerings also included the much admired 'Queen's cake', a particular favourite among children who enjoyed the different small shapes it came in—diamond, heart and flower-shaped. This was a simple sponge-like cake, lightly flavoured with vanilla or lemon and sometimes sprinkled with raisins. The small saanchas or moulds held the runny batter firmly in.

Our 'Trichonapoli' cake is a family heirloom and more like a mithai than a cake. In keeping with the South Indian town of Tiruchirapally after which it was probably named, it has plenty of fresh coconut. The recipe calls for sooji (cream of wheat), khoya (milk solids), grated coconut and sugar, flavoured with roasted cinnamon, green cardamom and nutmeg in equal measure. The sticky batter is spread in a thaali (flat plate), baked and then cut into diamond shapes, much like a barfi.

Back to our Christmas cake now gently perfuming the small room while things were put away and the tin trunks cleared out. The seniors would be fussing, worried that their precious cake would burn but the baker's decision was final. Once the cakes came out, they were allowed to cool down and then packed for the short trip home where they would be overturned on the dining table overnight to allow any moisture to dry out.

The next morning, they would be removed from their tins and packed neatly into metal trunks, covered with butter-paper, and set aside to be opened only on Christmas Day when they could be eaten and shared generously in the true spirit of the season. When you tasted your first slice of this honey-coloured cake, a staggering variety of fruits and nuts crumbling in every mouthful and the subdued aroma of spices filling your senses, you knew that Christmas hath truly arrived!

Armenian Christmas Food in Calcutta

~ Mohona Kanjilal ~

In Calcutta, many members of the Armenian community observe a customary fast in the week before Christmas and indulge only in light vegetarian meals for a week. The celebration begins with a late afternoon Mass on Christmas Eve, after which a Home Blessing ceremony is held at the Armenian College and Philanthropic Academy on Free School Street. A Christmas Eve dinner is arranged for the staff members and students of the institution which includes, among other traditional dishes, a customary pilaf with raisins and fish. The raisins in the pilaf represent the apostles. The Christmas Eve dinner known as 'Khetum' is a very important part of the traditional Armenian Christmas celebrations. Those observing the week-long abstinence from food, break their fast with this dinner. The Academy also serves the very popular Armenian Christmas pudding, anoush abour, made with wheat, berries and dried apricots.

The community celebrates Christmas on 6th January by attending Christmas Mass at the Armenian Church of the Holy Nazareth in the morning. This is followed by the festive lunch and traditional Armenian dishes occupy the family table. Meat is re-introduced after the short break in dishes like the dolma, a very traditional dish of ground meat and spices stuffed into grape leaves. Chopped onions, rice, butter, tomato paste, salt, black pepper and herbs are added to the minced chicken or beef. Warm water is added to this meat mixture and it is kneaded well. The grape leaves are boiled and very small portions of the mixture are put into them. The leaves are then rolled up like cigars. These are the dolmas.

A few grape leaves are put at the bottom of a pan and the dolmas are arranged on them. Water is poured into the pan to cover the dolmas and very little oil is added to the water, enough to give them shine. The dolmas are ready when the rice is thoroughly cooked. Another Christmas favourite is harissa, a porridge-like stew made with chicken. Also known as keshkeg, this stew is made by mixing shredded chicken, skinless wholewheat kernels and salt in chicken broth and bringing the liquid to boil on very low heat. When all the liquid is absorbed, the stew is then taken off the heat and the chicken and wheat are mashed till the dish resembles thick oatmeal. Harissa is served in bowls with dollops of butter on top and sprinkled with freshly ground cumin. The combination of warm harissa and lavash bread makes for a perfect winter dish.

Until the 1960s, it had been a customary ritual for community members to gather for a Christmas luncheon at the Armenian Club in Queens Mansion on Park Street after the church service was over. This was followed by a late afternoon tea party at the Armenian Sports Club on Mayo Road at the Maidan. The Armenian Club was once nicknamed Burra Club because all the prominent or 'burra' people from the community would go there. The luncheon menu would include, besides celebratory Indian and Anglo-Indian dishes, traditional pilaf with raisins, a fish preparation, dolma, salted white Armenian cheese and kebabs. It would be a contributory feast, with each family preparing a dish. Although this Christmas luncheon at the club has been discontinued, the tea party still continues, with community members carrying home boxes of Christmas cakes and goodies.

Though Christmas cake is not a part of the traditional Armenian Christmas menu, some members of the community celebrate with homemade cakes because of the influence of the English and Anglo-Indian customs. The delicious smell of baking and nutmeg pervades some Armenian homes during this festive season. There was a time when a considerable number of Armenian bakeries conducted thriving business in the city. They catered to the community and specialised in traditional sweets. Names such as Arizona and Minas come up as favourite haunts from where cakes were bought during the festive season. But after these bakeries downed their shutters in the 1980s, their cakes have been replaced with those from Nahoum's, Calcutta's famed Jewish bakery. Other standard features of both the Christmas Eve and Christmas spreads in most Armenian homes include cookies, baklavas, dried fruits and nuts.

Christmas Memories of a Family

A (Sort of) Christmas Miracle
~ *Nivedita Mishra* ~

Ask and you shall receive, seek and you shall find.

This was one of the earliest proverbs dinned into me as a child, and by now of course, its scope has expanded significantly but as a child below nine, the proverb proved to be true only at Christmas. For years, we would visit my maternal grandparents during the winter holidays and the highlight was the Christmas celebration—the ecstasy of knowing that with every bauble that went up on the evergreen conifer, the time for getting what you have asked for was coming closer! The 'ask' was invariably a couple of Enid Blyton books from the Wishing Tree, Famous Five or Malory Towers series, and obscene amounts of toffee, candy, jujubes and such.

While there was always a sneaky suspicion that Santa must have some sort of an agent in India who would go around locally on his behalf, there are a couple of incidents where I could have sworn I did hear bells and a booming 'ho-ho-ho' accompanied by a lot of rustling as he scrambled through his sack to look for what was earmarked for me.

My eighty-plus British great-grandmother, Grandma, would be the master of ceremonies that day—being both the most senior and most genuine Christmas mastermind. She would supervise the Christmas lunch with stuffed chicken if there was no turkey, a delicious gravy and sautéed vegetables. This was one occasion where she brought out her Mappin and Webb silver cutlery and made us feel particularly special—getting to use something that was meant to be a family heirloom that had come from 'phoren' shores.

Seen through my eyes, this was a rare day where all members of the Chatterjee clan managed to put aside their humongous amounts of intellectual and existential angst, put down their defenses and masks, and actually have fun. The finale was the perfunctory carol singing so we literally sang for our lunch as the entire family gathered around the piano, which my grandmother played to perfection, having given regular recitals broadcast on All India Radio at the time.

I often wondered if my Bengali Brahmin grandfather ever felt out of it, but looking back, I figure he had mastered his own ways to feel connected through his personal rituals throughout the year. Fish at least twice a day, a seven-kilometre walk, regular games of Bridge with his friends and a nightly massage with hot mustard oil provided him all the necessary armour and fuel to be a jolly good fellow right through.

Another highlight of the pre-Christmas days was the rehearsal food for the Delhi Christian Chorus. Since my mother was part of the choir and they performed annually, I was quick to overcome my resentment at being dragged along for rehearsals when I discovered the scrumptious food that the choir members brought to share, including the best-ever iced buttery Christmas cookies that the American choir director's wife made. It was a time when my taste buds were expanding their horizons, so, first tastes of chicken scandies, fruit cakes with marzipan icing, and fondants and fudges were being explored.

Time and tide saw many transitions, and with it, Christmas celebrations moved to my Uncle's where the arrangements were far grander and on a much larger scale, but entirely missing the 'it's just us Chatterjee family' feeling. An eclectic range of people from co-workers to artists and actors would be found making a beeline for my aunt's delectable roast leg of ham slow-cooked with pineapple.

Right from the arduous task of sourcing the ham from Gol Market, to the culinary marathon that ensued, starting with the alcohol-laced punch and ending with an equally rum-soaked Christmas pudding that seemed to stoke one's gastronomic fires yet again—the entire event seemed to happen in slow motion, and one went home knowing that it would be another three hundred and sixty-four days before one ate like that again!

Since growing up and moving on is an inevitability, part of my challenge was ensuring that I could successfully bring some of that Christmas cheer to my own home with my children. Having moved to the suburbs of Greater Noida from downtown Delhi with a one-year-old and two dogs, I was pretty much the embodiment of the harassed Mother India struggling to find the nearest accessible grocery shop and ensuring that her children were clean and fed.

Not much for keeping up with the neighbours who seemed to have some ritualised celebration every month, I found myself floundering in a haze of confusion among the *'Arre, aap Karwa Chauth nahin rakhti?'* (Don't you observe the ritual fast for your husband's well-being?) brigade. I had made up my mind that I would do a Christmas and Diwali celebration in my home so that my children got the best of both worlds and had some idea of what it is like to be multi-cultural. They already had some glimpses of the Oriya part of my father's family and the Maithil Brahmin traditions from their own father's side.

My first Christmas tree and a hoard of decorations

were actually given to me as a birthday present by a really thoughtful older friend with whom I had shared my concern about how I should start to create a tradition. My daughter was a year-and-a-half old and I clearly remember her mesmerised expression as the glittering, sparkling Christmas ornaments went up on the tree and I told her all about Santa and his presents. Sneakily though, I modified the proverb to 'Let's be happy with whatever we receive' in order to restrict excessive pressure on myself to try and get specific things for her from Delhi which was a feat to reach!

While I never really made a big deal about a traditional Christmas lunch, I continue to get my Christmas cake and cookies from Wengers in Central Delhi, which is authentic enough to feel like a Christmas miracle.

Speaking of miracles, there is something that happened around one Christmas which remains very much in our family stories as nothing short of a miracle. One of our two dogs had suddenly died leading to the other—Ustaad, a beautiful golden retriever—pining for him terribly. Ustaad had already lost the use of his back legs so could barely walk. All of us including the children were in deep mourning over both the loss of Janaab—our lovely Lhasa, and Ustaad's legs. We were all showing our anxiety in different ways, and my daughter, Fiza, and Ustaad seemed to cling to each other leaving Rushil at three confused and perplexed about where Jaanu Bhaiya had gone.

Almost a year had passed and Ustaad's overall health was declining rapidly. It was close to Christmas and on one of our visits to the vet, he advised that we should consider putting him to sleep so that he would finally be put out of his misery. Devastated, I mentioned this to my mother and she said she would pray for him with her prayer group and that I should leave the rest to God. Despite my avoidance of organised religion, a strong faith in God has really helped me through a lot in life. Exhausted, grateful and desperate for any help at all, I relented.

For the next three days, nothing happened and Ustaad's suffering, in fact, worsened. On the appointed day, my husband and I, both crying shamelessly, took our beloved forty-kilo darling down three flights of stairs on what was to be his last journey. As soon as we reached the vet and opened the back door to carry him out, Ustaad suddenly sprang up, got out of the car and went and dutifully did his business right on the vet's grassy lawn!

Our joy knew no bounds as we took him home, and were able to spend almost another full year with him before he passed away. Both the children were delighted and felt that they could not have asked for a more valuable Christmas present. While a part of me feels that Ustaad knew that I would crack up if I lost him so soon after Janaab, another part knows that it was really the power of that early proverb of truly seeking, asking and receiving proving its magic all over again.

~

Letting Go of Santa

~ *Rushil Mishra* ~

'No way!' shrieked my ten-year-old sister. 'There is no way you are going to tell Rushil about this!'

By now, I was very excited and all ears—ready to have my curiosity slaughtered as Mama sat me down and said very seriously, 'Rooey, I know this is going to come as quite a nasty surprise, but do you know there is actually no Santa, and I buy all those presents for you and put them under the Christmas tree before you wake up?'

I thought life was unfair enough with having an older sister who seemed to get the best and prettiest things but this was really the limit. I felt cheated and I wondered if this was some sort of conspiracy—there was actually no old man like that or did he simply think Indian kids were not special enough to make that long journey from the North Pole?

I consoled myself thinking that it really did not matter as long as I got the presents, but somehow, on discussing it with Fiza later, the image of my mother rushing around in a toy store trying to look for things within her budget was really quite pathetic. I also understood now why some of the presents were so carelessly packed and some so well—the ones that were well packed were actually gift-wrapped at the store or given by my grandmother Ai, who is a great packer, while my mother hates packing and would really much rather just give me the present as it is.

Fiza and I often discuss how one of the things about

Mama that always surprised us is her sudden jhatka approach to giving us reality checks. Though she is a loving mom and quite concerned about our feelings normally, when she suddenly decides something has to be done, she just goes ahead and does it, even at the cost of our 'childlike innocence'. This bee in her bonnet about suddenly getting Fiza to learn about the 'no Santa' deal meant that even I had to be told the harsh truth. And this was what my sister, for once, was trying to protect me from.

Christmas to me now has become a shared responsibility where Fiza and I are always fighting about who will get to do up the tree, and now that there is no Santa and we would rather choose our own presents, there is no drama about packing them anyway. I once asked Mama whether she never felt bad about taking Santa away from me at six. While what she said to me then did not make much sense, when I look back and see my friends all around me, there are bits about it that seem very true.

She explained to me that we already have so many good things in our life: a nice home, happy family, loving dogs, kind parents and many blessings that we take for granted that for us, Santa is something extra we can easily let go of. There are so many people and children around us who do not share our good fortune. They need to cling to Santa, and we should try to be a Santa for them sometime. It is not necessary always to give a gift-wrapped present for someone to feel loved and special. We can make them feel special by a simple gesture. By doing or saying something kind, or just being there for them when they need a friend.

As I grow up, I often think of this when my sister bullies me—it is withstanding her bullying that also gives me the strength to be a Santa for some other kids I know—friends whose parents fight a lot, or are generally having a rough time.

Feeling like I can be the helper rather than the one who needs help is very special, and I am glad I learnt it at Christmas.

(Rushil Mishra was eleven years old at the time of writing this essay.)

~

On Growing Up Through Christmas
~ Fiza Mishra ~

I can tell you without a doubt that I have grown up very randomly—with bursts of different cultures thrown at me by my crazy mum, who I felt could never make up her mind. So, she tried to give us a smattering of everything. From quite a cohesive understanding of my dad's Maithil Brahmin traditions, with their single-minded addiction to rich and varied non-vegetarian food and 'get completely sozzled' family get-togethers at our family home on a farm in north Bihar, to my mother's paternal Oriya family where despite knowing everything about them through her, it is always a struggle to follow the language and therefore communicate, and then all the mayhem in my head comes to a full stop when I think of Christmas, and I heave a sigh of nostalgia.

I have never actually had a white Christmas, but when I was about three and still the adored only child and apple of my parents' eyes, a new mall had opened up in Noida where they decided to recreate a white Christmas. I don't remember much of the details except for the feeling of floating on clouds as I was surrounded by white fluff, and my dad taking a picture of me with a snowman in the backdrop, with the carrot nose and everything.

The days leading up to Christmas before the 'Great Letdown' were always very exciting. For one, mum would seem extremely distracted and become suddenly very busy locking herself up in her room and doing a lot of things that were kept secret. While Rushil felt a bit neglected, I found it to be a nagging-free time when she did not ask me too many questions about school or homework and other boring details.

She was in a frenzy, always looking for the Christmas decorations for the tree, which she lost practically every year. It became a ritual of sorts where Rushil and I were tasked with climbing various lofts and hunting them down. Her stern voice would tell me, 'Fizz, you better remember where they are for next year, ok?' and me thinking, 'Yeah, right! Like I'm the adult who has to do your work for you and you go scot-free?'

One thing that never failed to surprise me was that if I ever asked her for something post-August, she would tell me to wait until Christmas since Santa would get it for me. I always felt hurt, thinking: if my own mother does not love me enough to get it for me then why should an old man from the North Pole bother? He already had enough on his plate with Rudolph and the jealous reindeer, didn't he?

I was probably the first person I knew who grew up in a family that celebrated Christmas with a tree and presents. My friends always did a lot at Holi and Diwali and Bhaidooj and their mothers made a big deal over Karwa Chauth with their glittering sarees and low-cut blouses. I never really felt bad when I saw my mother in her track pants watching the celebrations in other homes because Christmas was ours and it was special. It was the only time that I got quite a few of the things I wanted and there was a general air of festivity that lasted many days.

Soon, however, the Christmas trend caught on as did Valentine's Day and a specific day for every relative one had—obviously, social media and the greeting card lobby needed new fodder to live on.

I saw many other families bringing Christmas trees home and putting up some lights, but they never had the same depth as our Christmas did. Our Christmas was cozy—just the family and dogs—and it felt special. I admit there were huge bouts of jealousy when Rushil came into the picture and I felt the apple of my parents' eyes was cut in half, but there were also periods, as there still are, when I would be deeply grateful that all of their attention is not focused on only me.

I am not a believer, but when Ustaad sprang to life after my grandmother and her friends prayed for him, I did feel a huge sense of relief that after all, someone is watching over us.

The 'Great Letdown' was a biggie for me, and though I had always had my doubts, especially with the fake Santa Clauses in our school and in malls, knowing for sure that this was simply a fantasy was the end of my childhood in many ways. It taught me that there is always more to life than meets the eye. There is a story behind every spectacle, and a lot of effort goes on behind the scenes to put up a show.

It also taught me how we grow and evolve through traditions and how we relate to them. And whenever I think of our family rituals, the buck always stops at Christmas.

(Fiza Mishra was fifteen years old at the time of writing this essay)

Christmas Boots and Carols in Shillong

~ Patricia Mukhim ~

Christmas...the word triggers a whole host of activities in Meghalaya and other Northeastern states that have a predominantly Christian population. The Christmas fervour kicks in the moment the sun rises on 1st December. Most families would have saved enough to get the roof and walls of their houses painted after the long monsoon has taken its toll and left behind a residue of musty fungal patches. Nowadays, people have learnt to tackle this weather hazard by using tiles on the walls or even fungus-proof paint, but this was unheard of until the 1980s.

The next pre-Christmas ritual is to clean all the

windows and put up new curtains if you can afford it. Only after the house is given a facelift, follow the other preparations. Those who love the traditional Christmas fruit cake begin their baking by the first week of December, and the whole family joins in. But of course, the sultanas and other dried fruits have been soaked in rum since October so that they are plump and juicy and give the cake a zing that makes it no ordinary cake! Beginners may find their cakes sinking in the middle, but who cares! It tastes just as good and the aroma of rum makes up for a dent in the middle! Once the cakes are baked and cooled, they are stored in air-tight containers and will last through the year, to be served to friends who drop by during the Christmas season, and long after. The rum, I guess, is the preservative here.

By the second week of December, the Christmas spirit gains momentum. People begin to plan how to spend Christmas Eve. While the Shillong Club and Pine Wood Hotel offer a special Christmas bash, most families prefer to spend Christmas Eve with friends round a bonfire or just singing Christmas carols round the fireplace. This is also the coldest time of the year but the spirit of Christmas is such that even the cold does not deter people from coming out on the streets to sing Christmas carols. 'Jingle bells, jingle bells, jingle all the way...Oh what fun it is to ride on a one-horse open sleigh...Santa Claus is coming to town'. Sure, we don't have snow here and there's no way we can ride a sleigh but this has been a Christmas anthem for as long as I can remember. We like to imagine

Christmas as it is shown on those lovely Christmas cards we used to send to friends—nowadays, alas, the Christmas card that arrived by post has almost become extinct and greetings are exchanged on WhatsApp and Twitter!

There is a great rush among parents to get new clothes and shoes for the children, and for themselves. The main shopping centres at Police Bazar do brisk business, for it is also the season to buy woollens and warm clothing. Cardigans and coats flood the market, and those wishing to attend the midnight mass make sure they are well-covered from head to toe. Not forgetting the boots. Per capita, Shillongites must have the highest number of men, women, girls and boys wearing boots. There's certainly something about boots that appeals to the average person here apart from keeping our feet warm.

By the third week of December, from the 20th onwards, it's time to gear up and decorate the Christmas tree. In earlier days, we used branches of the pine tree which were sold by opportunistic peddlers. Today however, people are more conscious about not felling small pine trees or even the branches of larger pines and prefer store-bought artificial trees. Special stalls are set up in all the market places to sell decorations. The range is huge and gets better each year. Those who can afford it light up their compounds and hang fairy lights on trees in the garden. Everything looks like fairyland during Christmas. And the churches…oh how beautiful they look with those coloured lights and festoons! Who would not want to enter a church on Christmas Day to look upon Baby Jesus in his manger, and offer a silent prayer?

For many reasons but essentially because of Christ's pragmatic teachings, this season of goodwill also sees families that are otherwise in a cold war or friends who have not been at peace with each other for the rest of the year, let their guards down and choose to forgive and let go of past grievances. Somehow every hard feeling that one nurses against anyone or anything seems to melt away. It truly is a time of peace and goodwill.

This is both a spiritual and psychological healing process. How I wish that Christmas is celebrated more often so that we can have greater mental and spiritual healing.

These days, we have villages beyond the capital cities that take part in competitions about whose Christmas decoration is the best. A village in distant East Jaintia Hills called Moolamylliang is worth a visit. The whole village of about 200 households comes together to decorate the church compound and all the public spaces. The village people come forward and spontaneously contribute their mite for this annual jamboree. Many residents donate their time to physically clean up the village and put up the decorations a week ahead of Christmas, with the intent of attracting curious tourists to the village. Social media is a great facilitator and tourists flock to Moolamylliang in droves, enabling the villagers to earn a decent income from selling knicknacks and seasonal food to the visitors.

I have often been asked what happens in Shillong

during Christmas. In the past I have been diffident about telling them that Christmas has a purpose which for Christians is to celebrate the birth of their saviour. Hence, it's not just about revelry; there's also a spirit of quiet celebration and a tussle continues between those who believe Christmas is about loud music, song and dance, like New Year's Eve, and those who still cling to the old culture of worshipping Christ in a befitting manner by attending midnight mass.

And then as 24th December dawns, there is that impatience to celebrate with midnight services in different churches across the state. Church bells ring promptly at 10 p.m. so that the service ends at midnight and people are able to wish one another and exchange hugs. Tea and cakes await the worshippers outside the church. Hot tea is always welcome on a cold winter's night. And after the service, as people return home, the celebration begins....

We have been waiting for this for an entire year. The kids can't wait to open their presents which have all been nicely wrapped and kept under the Christmas tree. What a mad rush as the sound of wrapping paper being torn apart fills the air! And the surprise and excitement for the little ones who still believe that Santa Claus actually gave them what they asked for. Yes, parents tell their kids to write a small note to Santa and keep it in a little glass bottle, and they then quietly read their kids' wishes and buy them those gifts. But that's a well-kept secret until the children grow wiser, or learn not to believe in miracles (not always the best of lessons to learn).

Christmas is a time when invitations are not needed. Friends can land up at each others' homes any time on Christmas Eve to celebrate. Most friends drop by with a bottle of wine and others pool in the snacks and the party continues until the wee hours of morning. It's one day in the year when the state laws that noise should end at 10 p.m. is violated with gay abandon. Perhaps the cops too feel that people are entitled to a bit of noise that night... after all, it's Christmas. So the nightly silence is broken and the air rings with Christmas carols and soul, jazz and rock music. Nearly every fourth person in Shillong plays the guitar, so there's always music, and since nearly everyone sings, it's also a time to sing along, laugh and be merry. In fact, the sing-song sessions are what make Shillong a very special place on Planet Earth. Everyone from the chief minister down can strum the guitar and has a voice that could put lesser mortals to shame. And Christmas is also a day when all VIPism and formalities are set aside. You can land up at anyone's home and be welcomed in. It does not matter whether someone is the chief minister, a top cop, or the terrifying headmistress of your school.

Come 25th December, and the churches are filled to the brim. Even those who don't go to church on other days, choose to come and touch base with members of the congregation and join in the worship.

Another aspect that deserves mention is that Christmas is also a time when the purse strings are loosened. We are reminded, not least on social media, that Christmas is a time for giving rather than receiving. There are groups that visit orphanages and homes for the aged to spend time with the hapless and the abandoned. They take food or clothes for the orphans and sing carols along with them. Just to see the smiles on the faces of the elderly who otherwise are deprived of human company and to know that at least for a day, one has made a difference in their lives brings as much peace to the giver as to the receiver.

For tourists who want to experience the full spirit of Christmas, there's no better place than my city, Shillong, like which there isn't another place on Earth. Every hotel has a clutch of local singers who will entertain both residents and visitors until the cock crows. The air of festivity that one experiences here is absent elsewhere. That's why Christmas is also a time of homecoming. Almost all of those who work away from Shillong and its neighbourhood are drawn to their homes because Christmas reminds us that this is where we belong; where our spirit will always live.

I recall a time when my daughter Laetitia, who works and lives in Delhi, could not get leave for Christmas and how very lonely and lost she felt there despite being surrounded by friends. Christmas is about 'home' and all its means...a place where one is surrounded by loved ones; a place where one can unburden oneself; a place of peace and solitude that shuts out the noise of an impersonal world.

Christmas in Meghalaya does not end with 25th December. Every church organises a community feast in the church premises and all members and non-members are invited to this feast where members of the congregation collect donations, buy groceries and help in cooking and serving. This invitation is intended especially for those to whom life has not been kind. Church members donate so that the needy can have at least one good meal to celebrate Christmas; so that they too are reminded of a saviour who came to earth to be a friend of the destitute.

The Christmas spirit pervades not just Shillong but every nook and corner of the state and that spirit continues until New Year's Eve, when another round of celebrations begins. New Year's Eve also sees people keeping vigil as they did during Christmas Eve. It is only after New Year's Day has been celebrated that the Christmas tree is brought down, the decorations go back into boxes and the tree is packed and stored away until the next Christmas arrives.

October is almost bidding goodbye as I'm writing this. There is a nip in the air, November will soon arrive and bring with it the anticipation of the big day. It's time to get ready with the brooms and paint brushes to wipe away the ravages of the monsoon which has been almost interminable this year. It's time to give the walls a warm new look and to await the festive weeks when we all feel our burdens lifted, if only for a while. It's time to keep the list of songs ready for the Christmas Eve sing-song session. It's time to list out the homes we must visit to bring cheer to the ailing and the elderly, to see who among our neighbours needs our help during this season of compassion and to reach out to them. That is the true and enduring spirit of Christmas.

At this time of year all the FM radio stations play Christmas carols and there is a waft of Christmas songs from every passing vehicle. 'Come, sing it on the mountains/Over the hills and everywhere/Come, sing it on the mountains/For Jesus Christ is born'. This is one of my favourite carols and it seems to be a favourite of the FM stations too, for they play it the most after 'Jingle Bells...'

Merry Christmas!

An Indian Christmas Gallery

~ Various ~

'When we were children, around December 22 or so, my father would bring home a bunc of hay. And we knew it was time for our Christmas crib. There was a wooden frame who four walls slotted into each other; the front had hooks on which we hung the little angel There was the babe in the manger of course and his mother and father, the shepherds and th animals. The three kings would be placed some distance from the crib because they would arriv much later, on Jnauary 5. Our crib had a string of fairy lights buried in the hay and when was done, the lights would be turned off and we would ooh and aah at the sight. When I rea *101 Dalmatians* by Dodie Smith and one of the puppies—who is television mad, if I rememb right—sits in front of the crib in a meditative trance, I was taken back to that magic.

'The crib in the picture above comes out of Adivasi India. I bought it at a crafts fair Ranchi. Since then it has displaced all the other cribs—the wooden beauty I bought at the Bosto Museum, the Coptic Egyptian one, the tiny crib built into a nutshell from Budapest—becau it spells a Christmas in India for me and for all who look at it.'—Jerry Pinto

Photo credits: *Photography: Prerona Saikia; Lighting: Aboli Maharwade*
With thanks to SCMSophia for the time and space and resources to shoot this.

~

'Journey to Bethlehem'. Batik by P. Solomon Raj.

'Nativity', by comic book and animation artist Nishant Saldanha.

'Mary and Jesus', a painting by Sister Marie Claire.
(Courtesy: SMMI Provincialate, Bengalaru.)

'Adivasi Madonna', a painting by Jyoti Sahi.

Nativity scene by Goan artist Angelo da Fonseca.
(Courtesy: Xavier Centre of Historical Research, Goa.)

'The Three Wise Men Come Visiting', a painting by Sister Marie Claire.
(Courtesy: SMMI Provincialate, Bengaluru.)

'Mother Mary and Child Christ'. Mid-eighteenth century, late Mughal, Muhammad Shah period. National Museum of India, New Delhi. (Wikimedia Commons.)

Arogya Mata (Our Lady of Good Health), St Mary's Basilica, Bengaluru.
(Photo: Anthony Samson.)

Christ Church Shimla on Christmas Eve, 2020.

Christ Church Mussoorie lit up for Christmas.

Christmas decorations at CSI Church Kazhakootam, Kerala.
(Photo by Arunravi; Wikimedia Commons.)

A youth choir sings Christmas carols dressed in hijabs and skull caps in solidarity with fellow Indians protesting the Citizenship Amendment Act (CAA). Saint Thomas Mar Thoma Church, Kozhencherry, Kerala, 25 December 2019.

Famed Carnatic vocalist T.M. Krishna sings Tamil Sufi songs at Mumbai's Afghan Church during Christmas week.

Women's choir, Mahuapara Church, Chhattisgarh.

Streets of Aizawl decked up for Christmas. (Photos: Sharon Zadeng.)

Christmas week carnival in Dimapur.

Christmas lights at Sacred Heart Boys' High School in Santa Cruz, Mumbai.
(Photo by Sameer Pitalwalla; Wikimedia Commons.)

Devotees light candles on Christmas day at Sacred Heart Cathedral, Delhi.

Midnight mass at St. Paul's Cathedral, Kolkata.

Mary's Basilica, Bengaluru aglow with festive lights. (Photo: Ajith Kumar, Wikimedia Commons.)

Armenian Christmas Service at the Armenian Church of the Holy Nazareth, Calcutta.
(Source: A *Taste of Time: A Food History of Calcutta*, Speaking Tiger Books, 2021. Photo: Rangan Dat

A Father speaking at a unique celebration of Christmas Eve at the Ramakrishna Mission, New Delhi, 2007. (Photo courtesy PIB.)

All Saints Church in Akola, Maharashtra, on Christmas.
(Photo by Yogdes; Wikimedia Commons.)

Christmas Eve at the Worli BDD chawls, Mumbai, 2021. (Photos: Zaen Alkazi.)

Children dressed up as Santa Claus leave for school in Fazilka, Punjab.
(Courtesy: Ecocabs, Fazilka.)

Song Krittan, or Song Kristan, the ritual of open-air song and dance that heralds the end of Christmas and New Year celebrations in the Garo Hills. (Photo by Visham Thapa; Wikimedia Commons.)

Kuswar, the assortment of sweets and savouries distinct to Christmas in the Konkan region.

Rum and raisin cake of Flurys, the iconic cakeshop of Kolkata.

The Season of Hope in Chandigarh

~ Nirupama Dutt ~

It's that time of year again. Crimson poinsettias in small pots hold our gaze at nurseries all over the city, flaming red defiance at the dull haze in the air. Migrant hawkers, clothed in Coca Cola red, have been doing the hip-hop at traffic signals, waving Santa caps and bearded masks supposed to represent St Nicholas of Myra, who morphed into Santa Claus. His is the face of the man who has eaten well and has joy to spare, and although the malls are not as full as they used to be—the cash crunch and after-effects of the pandemic continue—Christmas is here. Never mind the slim wallets, there is still enough for a bite of a plum cake, a swig of rum and the earworm of a carol or two.

It is a matter of relief that despite the winds of religious polarisation that have been blowing now without pause, Christmas continues to be celebrated, everyone joining in, no matter what the faith of their birth. This convergence of faiths in festivity reminds me of a line from the novelist Nayantara Sahgal's *Storm in Chandigarh*: 'I am a Hindu by birth, a Christian by education and a Muslim by culture.' She spoke for many of us—who are not only Amar, Akbar and Antony but also Aradhna, Amiah and Annabelle, rolled into one. We contain multitudes and these multitudes call out every Christmas: 'Come and behold him.' For this is a birth, and women understand birth more than anyone else, understand that this is the present and the future—this could be Hope, and it must be celebrated and protected.

This gets me thinking: when was the Annabelle in me awakened, and which was the first Christmas of my life before I was suitably 'convented'? I think it was in 1959, when the city of Chandigarh was still in its childhood. My father took me, a four-year-old, that Christmas evening to wish the family of the Padri from Australia, who had recently come to live in a house just a plot away from ours. I, the little ugly duckling, was dumbstruck at the sight of the all-White family, the elegant wife of the clergyman and his two pretty teenage daughters dressed in slim skirts and Cashmere wool jumpers. My eyes opened wide when I saw in a corner of the living room a tall conical tree with a star shining on its tip and its green branches adorned with cotton snowflakes and shiny trinkets and tiny fairy lights. I still recall the look and the taste of the dates stuffed with walnuts and powdered with castor sugar that the younger daughter served us. I was overjoyed when she insisted that I take a second piece.

The next year, the first of the 1960s, the eldest of my six brothers, an educationist, returned after a year's stint in the Centralia School District of the US. The family had gone there by sea but they returned by air and all through that journey, my bhabhi held in her lap a cardboard box with fragile Christmas-tree decorations, spangled-glass bells and globes in different colours. As often happened in those days, their daughter, my niece, was a few years older than me. She made wonderful use of these decorations, along with cottonwool snowflakes and birthday-cake candles, so now we could have our own tree at Christmas time. Since our city had no firs and pines, she got my brother's colleague to fetch a small kikar tree; kikars grew aplenty in the wild empty plots all over Chandigarh. We continued this festive ritual till we were well into our twenties.

So it is I, Annabelle for a moment, who speaks to you. Annabelle wishes you a Merry Christmas. She is pained by a sketch of Santa Claus, her old buddy, which is doing the rounds of social media. He weeps over the lists he has been sent. So many children asking for bullet-proof vests. But Annabelle believes, with Carl Sandburg, that every baby is an expression of God's belief that the world should go on. It may be limping a little at this time but it will not always be so. Annabelle is too old to hope for a messiah, but like Vijay Tendulkar she also has 'an old belief in the youth'. She believes that this new generation will tire of division, anger and hate and then it will seek that which is best and most beautiful in all of us.

And so Annabelle's invocation is for joy and peace, as we sing our tappe and our boliyaan to the tune of camel bells on Christmas, and all the hundreds of other festivals of this land, this world.

Christmas Carols Punjabi Style

~ Translated by Nirupama Dutt ~

Tappe-boliyan *are improvised folk songs in Punjabi—couplets (*boliyan*) set to music based on the semi-classical* tappa *style and often accompanied by rhythmic clapping.* Tappe *were originally sung by camel riders in Punjab and Sindh to the music of the camel bells.* Boliyan *are usually traditional, passed down from generation to generation and elaborated along the way. But entirely new content has also emerged in recent times, reflecting changes in social realities and lifestyles. There are several Christmas-specific* tappe-boliyan *sung in Punjab and Punjabi communities around the world.*

Tappe by South Asian Women in Bethlehem Punjabi Church, New York

Aayi tappe di vaari ae
Mein kudi Punjabi Church di...

It is time for the contest of Tappe.
I, girl of the Punjabi Church,
Never lose in this singing game.

The angel comes to Mariam,*
Mariam trembles in fear:
What tidings has he brought?

The angel consoles Mariam,
'Mariam, have no fear
I come straight from God.

'Yesu has descended on earth,
You have given your all
To fulfil the will of the Lord.'

People wake from their sleep.
Hearing the angels' message,
The shepherds sing out in praise.

God has granted us this day
To deliver us from sorrow:
Yesu† has descended on earth!

---

*Mother Mary

†Jesus

Tappe-boliyan by the Well-known Gospel Singer Joshua Bashir of Lahore, Pakistan

Ik chamkeya taara ae...

A star shines bright
the dark world
bathes in His light.

He comes from the sky
bringing hope and joy
to all on Earth.

The Lord appears!
Iblees* and death
defeated forever!

Come let us thank him.
Bow our heads
before Yesu the saviour

Praise Him! Celebrate him!
Our first hope and our last
yesterday, today and tomorrow.

---

*The Devil

Made in India and All of That

~ Nilima Das ~

Of course, everything is made in India. We are geniuses at it and seeing, after all, is believing. Only a little observation yields dividends in the cultural syncretism around us. No doubt, this can happen in other countries too. Mark how pop icon Madonna sports a diamond nose pin and she does not live in India.

With a Bengali Hindu agnostic father and an English professional philosopher as a mother, the three Chatterjee children were in for some rare multicultural experiences. My early childhood is full of memories of Tulsi, our beloved ayah, feeding us seated on the floor on slats of wood called 'piris'. Then when I was five came the descent of our English maternal grandmother, an ardent Methodist, who on widowhood, was invited by our parents to join the family. She brought with her a Prestige pressure cooker which gave us plum pudding, plum cakes and a Christmas which was as much about delicious food as about receiving gifts.

It was the only festivity my mother took trouble over and she spent much thought preparing three pillowcases full of a variety of presents with always one orange tucked away in a corner. These bundles were neatly tied up and no matter how much we children speculated, we never found out where they were spirited away. Much excitement of anticipation was created, adding to the possibility of a Santa Claus who, we had heard, came down from the chimney. Throughout our primary years, we loved the much-awaited bundle placed carefully at the foot of each bed when we were in deep slumber. There were specially chosen gifts suited to our current interests...There was always a story book, a dress-length and dolls for the girls and possibly a length for a bush shirt for my brother with dinky toys. There must have been sweets, of course, probably bulls-eyes that we loved. The dress-lengths were eventually made up into frocks from Simplicity printed patterns that Grandma ordered from her sisters-in-law in England. There were two them, Taff and Bead, married to two brothers, Oliver and Stanley.

Later, in the fifties, when we were older, my mother completed her doctorate and had to leave for England for a year to do her post-doctoral studies. At the end of the year, she returned with a huge trunk full of gifts that would spread over several birthdays and Christmases. The trunk had to be shipped out, it was so huge. We children watched in wonder as she pulled out items for the current Christmas. There were poppet necklaces and Alice bands from Woolworths, cardigans from Marks & Spencer, permanent pleated skirts that had as yet not entered the Indian market and several lengths of material that would keep Grandma employed at her Singer sewing machine, the very same machine on which she had made all my mother's clothes as a girl.

Grandma's wardrobe in her bedroom was full of treasures like a chaffinch's nest with real eggs still preserved in it...Grandpa had sucked out the innards so the shell remained intact. He had been a great birdwatcher and this was a little memento from her past with him. Just thinking of our Christmas opens up a flood of memories. Grandpa, Norman Gantzer, had been a civil servant working under Curzon in British times. His office was in the Writers' Buildings, Calcutta. He met Grandma, the young Edith, when she was twenty-four at the home of some friends in England. He was on furlough and was a much older man, nearly thirty years older, we were told. They fell in love but Edith was adamant she would not leave her own country and he would have to resign from his job and come out to England to marry her. So, this is what he did. How Grandma managed on a retiree's pension and raised Margaret, our mother, is a lesson for marriages in India where the dowry scourge still follows brides everywhere. They bought and sold houses and managed to make a small margin of profit which was used for living expenses.

Young Margaret had to work for a scholarship to get into Grammar school. There were also piano lessons and she did music exams. Those were the war years and the child had to study in the trenches when London was being bombed. Then when she grew up more study was required to gain a scholarship to Somerville College, Oxford. There she got a PPE degree (philosophy, political science and economics). She met my father, N.N., at a debating club. He was sixteen years older and they came out to India to begin their married life. Perhaps the stories she had been told by her adoring father gave the twenty-year-old romantic notions of the glories of India. In her case, there was no hesitation of leaving her country. It was the height of the Independence movement and when we children came along, we were the first batch of 'midnight's children', a phrase made famous by Nehru from his first speech as prime minister of a free India.

Growing up meant Christmases we looked forward to with the fascinating contents of our pillowcases and the aromas of Grandma's cakes and puddings. I can see her sitting at the dining table cutting up the raisins with her scissors and de-seeding them, the sultanas were washed in boiling water and also spliced; there was colourful peel scissored into little pieces, walnuts that were rendered into crunchy bites, nutmeg to flavour, the right quantity of sugar beaten with eggs and the whole thing mixed and mixed with her wooden spoon to get the consistency for baking. Whichever child sat through this exercise got the chance to stick a forefinger into the bowl and lick off the leavings at the sides.

I do not remember any turkey, perhaps there was one sometime but usually we got a chicken roast. For this, there was special stuffing made with boiled potato, finely-cut chicken liver or kidney, nutmeg and basil flavouring. It was stuffed into the gaping chicken gut hole and firmly stitched up by Grandma with her long darning needle and strong thread before being inserted into her pressure cooker for the roast.

Grandma was a staunch Methodist and the three of us trooped along to church every Sunday. Our mother did the driving. She was not an observant Christian but her services were required to leave us at church. She also filled in when there was no organist. Being a seasoned broadcaster in All India Radio she played the organ with aplomb. I remember her 'Trumpet Voluntary' played with gusto. One Christmas, she trained the choir to sing an anthem. There were a few gifted soloists those days. Who can forget Robin Benjamin's dulcet rendering of 'Holy City' and Avinash Lall's rich baritone ringing out 'The Trumpet Shall Sound'? For several Christmases, she accompanied my 'How Beautiful Are Thy Feet' from Handel's 'Messiah'. I sang first soprano those days in the choir seated next to grandma.

There were no Christmas parties. Only what we got at Sunday school at church. What I remember is the special assemblies at school; there was one for Janmashtami, Eid, Gurupurab and Buddhpurnima, and there was one for Christmas as well. The school choir would sing 'Silent Night, Holy Night' and 'O Come All Ye Faithful' as misty-eyed and sincere as everyone else. We were, of course, all the same colour. I knew it was common that though we were all Indians, it was okay for each family to have its own religious festivals and customs.

The Christmas tree those days in the fifties was usually a branch of a casuarina tree my father got cut down from a forest. My mother would decorate it with tinsel and shiny multi-coloured baubles. As we grew older, we three would take over this job. At the foot of the tree and sometimes on the top of the piano we would place a pop-up depiction of the birth of Christ in a manger. On Twelfth Night the decorations would be removed and carefully packed in a biscuit tin to be preserved for the next year. Each of us had to set aside a little pocket money to buy something for the poor, usually a box of coloured pencils and we would take this to church to place at the foot of the large tree there done up with coloured lights.

My socialist mother who was a Gandhian scholar and wore khadi sarees did not give us any doctrinal teaching as she wished us to think for ourselves.

Many years later when churches no longer had English priests and brown-skinned priesthood took over, I attended the marriage of a young priest. He mounted the dais wearing a suit and tie with his white-gowned bride at his side; then when all the present-giving was over, he descended with his bride for a costume change and emerged, hey presto, with a brocade galaband and his wife in a red saree! When they mounted the dais again there was an exchange of jaymala. I faced the bridegroom with what I thought was an anomaly and he replied, unperturbed, 'Indian Christians are allowed jaymala.' I reasoned, sringar is after all the Sanskrit for love; red also signifies sringar, so Indian brides may wear red.

There are changes. After all, Archies, the multinational, had stepped on our shores. Valentines are rapidly replacing rakhis so girls no longer have to coyly tie strings on fake bhaiyyas (brothers), but can actually acknowledge their attraction. And goon squads who have not realised that skin-tight jeans and jeggings are manufactured in factories in Jalandhar and are rapidly replacing the salwar and kameez, will get the lesson of their lives if jean-clad women bust them on their heads with their Gucci handbags when they are caught dating. See where a little thought gets you!

As a coiner of words, I came up with the idea that 'Christianism' in our churches is after all, a kind of 'Hinduanity'. No wonder it is said that Hinduism has great absorbent power. It is inclusive for after all, a great saint like Ramakrishna had visions of Christ. One old neighbour of mine nodded when I told her I was 'Issai' and said, '*Girja me bahut shakti hai. Woh bhi bhakti hai.*' (The church has great power. That too is worship.)

Alas, growing up came to an end and then after a

Master's degree, marriage inevitably happened. This was a rite of passage into a new life with a fellow M.A. in English from Delhi University. My marriage ceremony was predictably complex. My baptised sister insisted on a Christian blessing so although I married a Hindu, he was as nominal a Hindu as I was a nominal Christian. We had the Christian blessing at the Cambridge Brotherhood in Kashmiri Gate in Delhi. I chose a white kanjeevaram saree with a red border to give a Bengali touch and a friend arranged for a big bouquet of red roses. Then we had a Hindu ceremony in Kolkata. I chose a carmine red Benarasi silk saree with an oxidised gold border. My cousin sister decorated my cheeks with tiny dots of sandalwood paste ending with one curlique on each cheek. Proud of all my regalia, including borrowed earrings, I presented myself to my mother for a word of appreciation. Her sole item of jewellery was a wedding ring. She looked at me and declared, 'Oh, you look like a Christmas tree!'

A Christmas Prayer

~ Words and Music by Alfred J D'Souza ~

~ Arranged for Choir by Leon deSouza ~

1

Play on your flute
Bhaiyya, Bhaiyya
Jesus the saviour has come.
Put on your ghungroos
Sister, Sister
Dance to the beat of the drums!
Go find your kinsmen in the rice fields,
Seek them harvesting the crop.
Look for your women in the market,
Hear them gossip while they shop.
Run into their throng
Sing your happy song,
Spread the good news of his birth,
Let its joyous sound
Echo all around, till it
Covers the ends of the earth!
Till it covers the ends of the earth!
It covers the ends of the earth!
Ah! Ah!

2

Play on your flute
Bhaiyya, Bhaiyya
Jesus the saviour has come.
Put on your ghungroos
Sister, Sister
Dance to the beat of the drums!
Light up a deepam in your window
Doorstep, don with rangoli
Strings of jasmine, scent your household
Burn the sandalwood and ghee,
Call your neighbour in, smear vermillion
Write on his forehead to show
A sign that we are one
Through God's eternal Son
In friendship and in love ever more! (3)
Ah! Ah!

About the Contributors

Nazes Afroz is former executive editor, BBC World Service, South and Central Asia. An independent writer, photographer and translator, he is currently based in New Delhi. His latest book, *In a Land Far from Home: A Bengali in Afghanistan*, is a translation of the memoir of the noted Bengali writer Syed Mujtaba Ali. Afroz's photography works have been exhibited in three continents.

Minoo Avari is a retired tea and coffee planter who lives in Kodaikanal. President of the Mya Palanimalai Farmer's Association (MPFA) for several years, he is also president of the United Citizen's Council of Kodaikanal and the Council Protection Association. He writes and plays tennis in his spare time.

Jane Borges is a Mumbai-based journalist and novelist. She currently writes for the *Sunday Mid-day*. Her debut novel, *Bombay Balchão*, was published in 2019.

Arul Cellatturai was a Tamil poet and engineer who published his first book in the devotional genre, Pillaitamil, in 1985.

Nilima Das has been a PGT in English in leading public schools. She did a module on Art Education for her M.Ed which led to developing an interest in Indian folk art. She has published a book of poems ,'My Roots'; has done content writing for two websites, Lotushighlights, a direct selling company that is Asia's largest distributor for The World Book Encyclopaedia, and Elt.emacmillan on poetry appreciation worksheets for teachers of English. Now retired, she does in-service training for teachers, freelance journalism, and enjoys singing in her spare time which led to her performing in ten opera productions for the Neemrana Music Foundation. She has a married daughter and two grandchildren.

Priti David was born in Allahabad and moved to Hyderabad when she was ten years old. She did a BA (Honours) in Economics from Lady Shri Ram College, Delhi. Priti pursued Bharatanatyam with danseuse Leela Samson for many years. She has been a journalist with *The Economic Times* and BBC World and worked with the Crafts Council of India. She also taught at St Joseph's Boys' High School, Bengaluru and Rishi Valley School. She has now returned to writing and editing and focuses on stories from rural India, education and the outdoors.

Nirupama Dutt is a poet, journalist and translator based in Chandigarh. She writes in Punjabi and English. Her published work includes *The Ballad of Bant Singh: A Qissa of Courage*, a biography; *Ik Nadi Sanwali Jahi* (A Stream Somewhat Dark), a book of poems, for which she received the Punjabi Akademi Award; and *Lal Singh Dil: Poet of the Revolution*. She has also translated and edited an anthology of Punjabi fiction, *Stories of the Soil*; an anthology of fiction by Pakistani women writers, *Half the Sky*; and a collection of resistance literature from Pakistan, *Children of the Night*.

Mohona Kanjilal was born in Kolkata and spent most of her childhood in Bengaluru. She is an alumnus of Loreto College, Kolkata and she began her career in the city as a freelance journalist. Mohona is the author of *A Taste of Time: A Food History of Kolkata* (2021) and two short story collections.

Mary Sushma Kindo is a domestic worker in Delhi and is currently employed in a house in South Delhi. She hails from the village of Simdega Sawai in the Simdega district of Jharkhand.

Easterine Kire is a poet, novelist and writer of short stories and children's books. She is the first Naga writer to publish an English novel, titled *A Naga Village Remembered*. In 2011, she was awarded the Governor's Prize for Excellence in Naga Literature and the Free Word by Catalan PEN, Barcelona in 2013. She is also the winner of the Hindu Prize, the Gordon Graham Prize for Naga Literature, the Tata Literature Live Award for Fiction, and the national Sahitya Akademi's Bal Sahitya Puraskar.

Elizabeth Kuruvilla is Executive Editor, Penguin Random House India. She has previously worked as a journalist with newspapers and magazines such as *The Hindu, Mint, The Indian Express* and *Open* magazine. She has been the books and arts editor at several of these publications and was also the editor of the international art newspaper, *Blouin Art info*.

Damodar Mauzo is a prolific Goan short story writer, novelist, critic and script writer. He has over fifteen books to his credit and his work has been translated into various Indian languages besides Portuguese, French and English. The national television channel, Doordarshan, has telecast two of his acclaimed stories in the Hindi serials *Ek Kahani* and *Aur Ek Kahani*. He was awarded the Sahitya Akademi Award in 1983 for Konkani for his novel *Karmelin*; the Vimala V. Pai Vishwa Konkani Sahitya Puraskar for his novel *Tsunami Simon* in 2011; and India's highest literary honour, the Jnanpith Award, in 2021.

Vivek Menezes is a widely published writer and photographer, the co-founder and co-curator of the Goa Arts and Literature

Festival, founding editor of *The Peacock* daily newspaper, the International Film Festival of India, columnist for *Dhaka Tribune* and *Scroll.in,* and a frequent contributor to other leading periodicals. As three-time curator at the Serendipity Arts Festival, he was responsible for the large-scale group exhibitions, *Konkani Surrealism* (2017), *Panjim* 175 (2018) and *Mundo Goa* (2019). He lives in Panjim with his wife and three sons. Vivek is currently working on a book on the cultural history of Goa.

Fiza Mishra is now pursuing her undergrad degree in Sociology from Ashoka University. A born feminist, reader, and equal rights advocate, Fiza has moved through many genres ranging from Indian mythology to the classics. Her current fascinations include exploring contributions made by lesser-known female activists in South East Asia. Her forays home include entire days spent in the kitchen rustling up exotic recipes and she occasionally condescends to watch Netflix with her family despite pointing out everything that is politically incorrect.

Nivedita Mishra is a former investigative journalist, documentary filmmaker, skincare brand owner, alternative healing therapist and communications manager. She now runs www.gopangolinstudios.com, helping brands and start-ups to communicate their best stories across platforms.

Rushil Mishra loves making friends and increasing his 'influencer' base. An avid fan of the World Wrestling Entertainment matches, he plays football and chess and is a big fan of Lionel Messi. Fond of coming up with one-liners to amuse and outsmart the older generation, Rushil is confident that he has a lot to contribute to the world—as long as they listen and are not 'toxic'.

Patricia Mukhim is a social activist, writer, journalist and the editor of *Shillong Times*, known for her activism and her writings on mining in Meghalaya and Khasi people of the state. She is a recipient of honours such as the Chameli Devi Jain award, ONE India award, Federation of Indian Chambers of Commerce and Industry FLO award, Upendra Nath Brahma Soldier of Humanity award, North East Excellence award and the Padma Shri (2000). Patricia is the founder of Shillong, We Care, a non-governmental organization involved in the fight against militancy in Meghalaya.

Mudar Patherya is a businessman, Urdu lover, butterfly-chaser, stock-picker and writer. He runs Trisys, India's oldest agency—and among the largest—in the area of corporate financial communications. Mudar is also a prominent activist in Kolkata (urban, environmental and social). He inspired the creation of a philanthropic NGO called Kolkata Gives that mobilized nearly a hundred million rupees during the Covid-19 pandemic for those in need.

Veio Pou is the author of *Waiting for the Dust to Settle* (2020), which won the Gordon Graham Prize for Naga Literature (Fiction category) 2021. He teaches at Shaheed Bhagat Singh College, University of Delhi, and likes to engage on issues that relate to literature, culture, society and faith.

Anupama Raju is a poet and literary journalist. Her books include the poetry collection *Nine*, and the novel *C*. Her poetry has been featured in several anthologies, including the *HarperCollins Book of English Poetry*, *The Yellow Nib Modern English Poetry by Indians* and *Prakriti*. Her writing has also appeared in *Poetry at Sangam*, *The Hindu*, *The Caravan*, *Indian Literature*, *Mint Lounge*, *Pratilipi* and *The Little Magazine*, among others. She also translates poetry and short fiction from Malayalam to English.

Paula Richman is a Professor of South Asian Religions at Oberlin College. She specialises in the study of the *Ramayana* and Tamil language and is the editor of several books including, *Many Ramayanas: The Diversity of a Narrative Tradition in South Asia*. She speaks and reads several languages, including Sanskrit, and has travelled throughout India for more than three decades. She is the recipient of a Guggenheim fellowship and several grants from the National Endowment for the Humanities and the American Institute of India Studies.

Deborah Rosario obtained her doctorate in English from Oxford University and spent the next few years teaching and supporting research projects in Oxford and Mumbai. She also worked as the National Coordinator for the UK at the Veritas Forum. Deborah is now a Senior Education USA Adviser at USIEF Mumbai. Over the years, she has written on books, art and film, and memoirs of her community.

Jaya Bhattacharji Rose is an international publishing consultant who has been associated with the publishing sector since the early 1990s. She has worked with several publishing houses as an editor and a content expert. Her blog has crossed 7.6 million visitors. Ace Literary Consulting, the literary agency that she co-founded, represents writers across genres. Jaya is as passionate about cooking as she is about books. Her mother encouraged her to be in the kitchen at a very young age and she did the same with her daughter. Sharing food recipes and histories is an integral part of Jaya's existence.

Manimugdha S. Sharma is pursuing a Ph.D. in History at the University of British Columbia, Vancouver, Canada, and is the author of the book *Allahu Akbar: Understanding the Great Mughal in Today's India* (2019). Before beginning his doctoral journey, he was a journalist in New Delhi where he spent fifteen years between *The Times of India*, *Hindustan Times* and *The Indian Express*. He tweets at @quizzicalguy and enjoys long conversations over cups of coffee.

Hansda Sowvendra Shekhar is a doctor and the author of the acclaimed collection of short stories, *The Adivasi Will Not Dance*, which was shortlisted for The Hindu Prize; and the novel *The Mysterious Ailment of Rupi Baskey,* which won the Sahitya Akademi Yuva Puraskar and was nominated for The Hindu Prize, the Crossword Book Award and the International Dublin Literary Award. His last published work was the novel, *My Father's Garden* (2019), which was shortlisted for the JCB Prize. Hansda has written a novel for children titled *Jwala Kumar and the Gift of Fire: Adventures in Champakbagh.* He also translates prose and poetry from Santhali and Hindi into English.

Copyright Acknowledgements

The editors and publisher thank the following for permission to reproduce copyright material:

Mohona Kanjilal for 'Armenian Christmas Food in Calcutta', excerpted from *A Taste of Time: A Food History of Calcutta*, Speaking Tiger Books, 2021.

Minoo Avari and *Kodai Chronicle* for 'Yuletides of Yore', excerpted from *Between Heaven and Earth: Writings on the Indian Hills*, edited by Ruskin Bond and Bulbul Sharma, Speaking Tiger Books, 2022.

Paula Richman for 'Moon 1' and 'Moon 3: Difference', her translations of poems by Arul Cellatturai, excerpted from *Extraordinary Child*, University of Hawai'i Press, 1997.

Easterine Kire for 'Did Your Christmas Cake Come Out of an Ammunition Box Too?' which was first published in the *Eastern Mirror*, Nagaland, 23 December 2013.

Vivek Menezes for 'I'm Dreaming of a Goan Christmas'. A version of this essay first appeared in *Mint Lounge* as 'Christmas in Goa Encompasses the World with Great Felicity' on 25 December 2021.

Manimugdha S. Sharma for 'Christmas: How India's Pluralistic Past Shows the Way Forward', version of which first appeared in *The Assam Tribune* on 25 December 2021.

Every effort has been made to trace copyright holders and to obtain their permission for the use of copyright material. The publisher would be grateful if notified of any omissions or errors that should be corrected in future reprints or editions of this book.

www.ingramcontent.com/pod-product-compliance
Lightning Source LLC
LaVergne TN
LVHW020410070526
838199LV00054B/3577